RUNES

RUNES

DIVINE SYMBOLS OF PROPHECY

ANDREW McKAY

SIRIUS

SIRIUS

This edition published in 2023 by Sirius Publishing, a division of
Arcturus Publishing Limited,
26/27 Bickels Yard, 151–153 Bermondsey Street,
London SE1 3HA

ISBN: 978-1-3988-2097-5
AD008725UK

Printed in China

CONTENTS

CHAPTER ONE

WHAT ARE RUNES?

Runes are found throughout much of Northern Europe. From those carved into runestones – great boulders that tell tales of Norse fame and fortune – to simple inscriptions on weapons and possessions, these ancient symbols are a testament to man's desire to learn, to understand and to explain. As well as telling us much about the lives of those who came before us, they can also help us to divine where we should go next.

Our journey into runes starts with a fork in the road, as there are debates about the meaning of the word itself. It is often associated by scholars with words such as scratch or carve, which makes sense linguistically, as it describes how the runes come to be inscribed on their materials.

However – as in English, where few words have only one meaning – the word rune has several other readings. One of these is 'inscription', which means that the word doesn't refer to a single character but

to one incidence of writing. While this is technically correct, it's probably not really a useful distinction outside of academic runology so I shall be using the word 'rune' in the way that most people would understand it – to mean a single character. I will use either 'runes' or 'runic inscription' to refer to a set of characters strung together into what we would call words, sentences and paragraphs.

If we refer back to earlier languages such as Old Norse and Old English, rune has another meaning of 'holding a secret'. This is where we get our ideas about runes as being somehow magical and part of the mythology of the Norse people. The source materials for Norse mythology – particularly the Icelandic *Edda*, which we will discuss further later on – certainly attest quite strongly to a mystical aspect and origin of the runes.

Academics will probably tell you that runes are nothing more than a forerunner to today's letters, but modern rune users, and those who attempt to keep alive the secrets of the Norse and Germanic mythologies, tell a different story. They believe the runes were a secret connected with fate, handed to man through the gods, and they are still a powerful spiritual channel that can help us divine information about the world and our place in it.

The curious thing about both sides, however, is that neither has definitive proof. A sceptic might tell you that casting runes has no logical bearing; their arrangement is only defined by random chance. But if you ask someone who has found help in decision making through using runes, they will probably tell you that the stones are indeed special and mystical.

The conflict between the academic and the mystic around runes is perhaps understandable.

Those who believe in academic rigour might scoff at concepts involving higher powers and mythology, while those who use runes in a divine context might not wish to engage with those who might ridicule them. But I honestly believe that both sides can learn a lot from each other and that an understanding can grow from a common interest in runes.

There is a third way to understand runes, which is that the 'magic' at work is the concentration of the mind on what one truly thinks and desires, which in turn manifests the outcome that the caster desires. If you use runes and you find that your life improves because of them, does it really matter whether you choose to believe that it was divine inspiration, or the power of suggestion that helped steer your subconscious to the right path?

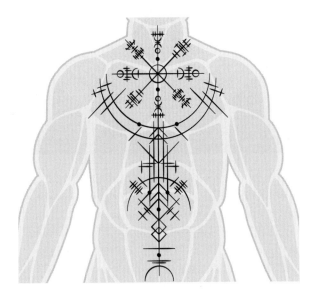

So join me as I attempt to show how the two sides are not necessarily as far apart as they may seem. On this journey, I aim to weave a path through the spiritual and the academic aspects of runes to see how, ultimately, the two worlds can exist together. The story of runes is too often told from only one side but I hope to blend the mystical and mundane into one coherent whole.

I shall start out with how the scholars believe the runes developed, and the different systems of runes that we know about. I'll give you some information on what we know, and don't know, about the history of the runes as human inscriptions as well as how runes are still in use today, even though that might be in ways that are contentious. After that we'll dive deeply into the world of divination and how people believe the runes can still be a powerful force in daily life.

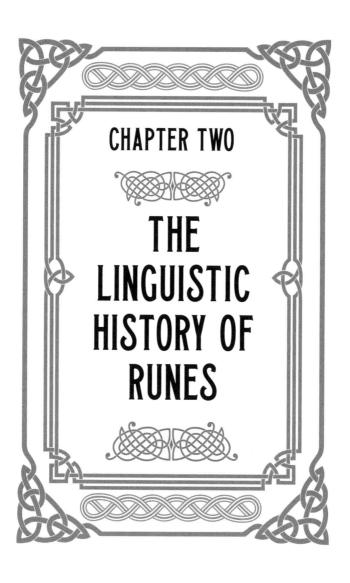

CHAPTER TWO

THE LINGUISTIC HISTORY OF RUNES

One of the biggest problems with history is that we know almost nothing about it. Out of all that can be known about the happenings of the human past, the amount we do know is closer to zero than we like to admit.

It seems odd that in the current age, where we have all known information at the touch of a smartphone screen, there can still be so much we don't know. How can this be? Well, primarily it's because, for the majority of what we now call human history, no one was taking notes.

Stories were passed down through the generations in the oral tradition. Mothers and fathers would sit around and tell their children the great stories that were told by their parents, that they in turn learned from their parents.

One big problem with oral histories is that they change over time. Through several generations of a tale, a man who is taller than average might become

Oral histories were all humans had before the advent of writing.

a ten-foot-tall giant. A large whale might become a ship-destroying monster that strikes fear into the heart of the hardiest Vikings.

It was only with the development of writing systems that our ancestors could start to store knowledge and preserve histories precisely. The

Early writing, such as Egyptian hieroglyphics, were based on pictures.

best theory at present is that writing developed independently in at least four different places. Mesopotamia, Egypt, China and South America all have early writing systems – so different it's almost impossible that they are related to each other.

The very first writing systems were based on glyphs, or simplified pictures of objects, like Egyptian hieroglyphics, probably the most well-known example. Mostly these glyphs would have been used to keep track of things like livestock and produce. This worked well for a long time, as in many ways pictures can tell a story more easily than words. They are also easier for people to understand. If you show an uneducated man a picture of a bird, he will know instantly what it is. Show him the word 'bird' and he would have no idea.

Over time, there was a need to develop writing systems that mimicked the sounds used in speech so that more complex and precise concepts could be recorded and passed on. Names, for example, are difficult to explain with simple pictures, unless everyone is named after an object. This is where runes come in.

As one of the earliest writing systems in Northern Europe, runes and runic objects can tell us much about the people and how they lived at the time the inscriptions were made. The runes are primarily an 'alphabetic' writing system, meaning that the characters represent individual sounds, known to linguists as phonemes.

The rune characters also have names, and these names are often used to express ideas and concepts in their own right. This will become important later on, when we look into the modern usage of runes in divination, but it also presents problems when trying to translate runes, firstly into the old languages and from there into English. If a single rune can stand for either the letter 'e' or the concept of a horse, there's plenty of room for confusion in the translation.

Could runes have developed from the Etruscan alphabet?

The runes definitely evolved from what we call the Old Italic writing systems that developed in Italy in the last millennium BCE, which were themselves developed from the Ancient Greek alphabet. However, no one has been able to say definitively which system the runes developed from as there are similarities and differences between the runes and each of the old writing systems.

One answer is that they developed from the Etruscan alphabet – the known ancestor of the Latin alphabet that most of us use in Europe and the Western world today. It's also possible that they developed directly from the original Latin alphabet itself as all of these early Italic and Latin alphabets date back earlier than the runes.

We have been able to rule out some possibilities, such as direct derivation from the Greek alphabet via the Goths, because the timelines make it impossible. In fact, the Gothic alphabet, used by the Greeks to translate the bible, contains two characters that most likely came from the runes as no other origin can be found.

We also don't really know how the runes travelled from Italy to Germany and Scandinavia. One thing we do know is roughly when it must have happened. The earliest known runic inscriptions date from around 150 CE in Denmark and Northern Germany. One of the biggest problems is that no artefacts have been found that definitively show exactly when the system first developed. If artefacts did come to light then we could enhance our knowledge of when and how runes evolved, but the chance of this is slim.

There's a strong likelihood that the writing system came to the Germanic people through war, perhaps from the Elbe watershed in West Germany or via East Germany in a Gothic route. However it arrived, there's a strong chance that the exchange of knowledge was accompanied by bloodshed.

Through careful study, we have managed to glean a lot of information about the rune characters, the sounds they likely represented, the meanings behind them and their place in the writing systems that used them.

While it's an alphabetic writing system, we don't use the word alphabet to describe the rune systems. Instead, we have the word Futhark. You may have seen this word if you've done any reading on runes before. But what does it mean and why do we use it?

CHAPTER THREE

INTRODUCING
THE
FUTHARKS

If we talk about 'the runic alphabet', we're being imprecise in two different ways. Firstly, although runes are an alphabetic writing system, they are collectively part of a futhark or fuþark, pronounced foo-thark, rather than an alphabet. That's because the word alphabet represents the first two characters of a writing system: 'alpha' and 'beta', from Greek, or 'aleph' and 'beth' from Hebrew.

In a similar way, Futhark represents the first six runic characters: 'f', 'u', 'th', 'a', 'r' and 'k'. The rune 'Thurisaz' is now transliterated as 'th', but was originally a single character, þ, that was used in all of the Germanic languages at one point. It was lost from most languages, including English, but is still used in Modern Icelandic.

Secondly, unlike our English alphabet of 26 characters, the runes are not a single futhark but at least three. The original futhark that was in use from the 1st century CE until around the year 700 is

known as the Elder Futhark. This then developed in two different ways. The Anglo-Saxon branch of the runes developed into the futhorc, with the o and c representing changes in how letters were pronounced between Norse and Anglo-Saxon. In Scandinavian countries the Elder Futhark became the Younger Futhark, which in turn developed in two distinct ways.

THE ELDER FUTHARK

Also known as the Older Futhark or Germanic Futhark, the Elder Futhark is the earliest set of runes that we have found, and experts believe it's the origin of all of the runic systems that came afterwards.

It consists of 24 characters, commonly arranged as three sets of eight, known as ætt (singular) or ættir (plural). The word ætt comes from the Old Norse word meaning a clan, group or family. This suggests that the runes in each set of eight are related to each other in some way. Linguists have failed to find a definitive answer to this so the reason for the groupings remains unclear.

The 24 runes of the Elder Futhark are:

ᚠ	ᚢ	ᚦ	ᚨ	ᚱ	ᚲ	ᚷ	ᚹ
f	u	þ/th	a	r	k	g	w
ᚺ	ᚾ	ᛁ	ᛃ	ᛇ	ᛈ	ᛉ	ᛊ
h	n	i	j	ï, æ	p	z	s
ᛏ	ᛒ	ᛖ	ᛗ	ᛚ	ᛜ	ᛞ	ᛟ
t	b	e	m	l	ŋ	d	o

As you can see, writing the word rune, we would get something like ᚱᚢᚾᛖ.

The first sequential listing of the Elder Futhark came in the form of the Kylver Stone in Gotland.

Dating to 400 CE, the listing is complete apart from
the 'ᚷ' and 'ᛈ', which are only partially complete. We
have enough sources, however, to be sure of what
they were.

In some sources the 'o' and 'd' runes swap places
and in some the 'i' and 'p' runes swap places. The
Vadstena bracteate, discovered in the town of
Vadstena in Sweden in 1774, contains an almost-
complete inscription. The medal was nearly
melted down by a goldsmith, but he was stopped
by a local clergyman who recognized the significance
of the item.

Bracteates were thin medals or coins, usually
of gold, that were worn on a necklace, possibly as
an amulet. They are divided into types, based on
the imagery contained on them. The centre of the
Vadstena bracteate includes an image of a man with
a four-legged animal, making it a C-type bracteate.
This is commonly attributed to Odin in Norse
iconography. There's also a bird that is separated by a
line. Around the edge is an inscription that reads:

TUWATUWA; FUÞARKGW; HNIJÏPZS; TBEMLNŌ[D]

The 'd' rune has to be assumed because it is
covered by the necklace holder. This is, however,
confirmed by an identical bracteate found in 1906 in

Motala where the necklace holder covers the 't' rune. The tuwatuwa has not yet been deciphered and may never be. The rest is clearly the Elder Futhark with the four letters swapping places as mentioned above.

The Elder Futhark is the one most associated with divination as it's the oldest, and therefore assumed to be the most closely associated with the Norse gods. We'll see the story of Odin and how he came to know the runes a little later on.

THE YOUNGER FUTHARK

Some time around the 8th or 9th century, the Younger Futhark – also known as the Scandinavian Runes – developed in modern Scandinavia. The Younger Futhark is a cut-down version of the Elder Futhark, consisting of only 16 characters.

Ironically, this happened at the same time as the actual language was expanding. So, we have a situation where there are more sounds in the language and fewer characters to represent them.

The Younger Futhark is further divided into 'Long Branch' runes, favoured in Denmark, and 'Short Twig' runes, favoured in Norway and Sweden. The characters are roughly similar to the Elder Futhark and are still grouped into three ættir, although as we will discover later, some of the meanings have changed.

The 16 runes of the Younger Futhark are:

ᚠ	ᚢ	ᚦ	ᚬ	ᚱ	ᚴ
f/v	u/v/w, y, o, ø	þ, ð/th	ą, o, æ	r	k, g
ᚼ / ᚽ	ᚾ / ᚿ	ᛁ	ᛆ / ᛅ	ᛋ / ᛌ	
h	n	i, e	a, æ, e	s	
ᛏ / ᛐ	ᛒ	ᛘ	ᛚ	ᛦ	
t, d	b, p	m	l	R	

As you can see, the first ætt loses g and w. The sound of the 'a' rune changes so it's now transliterated as a few slightly different sounds. The second ætt loses the old ï/æ and the p and the old j rune changes sound to become an a or æ. The z rune appears to turn on its head and move all the way to the end of the row where it's now transliterated as R. Finally, the third ætt lost the e, ŋ, o and d runes. The m rune has transformed into something similar to, but different from, the old z rune.

ᚹᚢᚦᚨᚱᚹ   ᚼᚾᛁᚼᛂ   ᛏᛒᛦᛚᛌ
ᚹᚢᚦᚠᚱᚹ   ᛏᚼᛁᛁ'   ᛁᚠᛏᛌ'
fuþąrk   hnias   tbmlʀ

    This shows the difference between Long Branch
(top) and Short Twig runes.

    The Younger Futhark was in use during the
Viking age, and so all Viking artefacts with runes
bear characters from the Younger Futhark. While the
Long Branch and Short Twig runes were favoured
in Denmark and Norway/Sweden respectively,
inscriptions containing both kinds of runes have
been found throughout the region.

    Finally, we also need to mention the staveless
runes of Hälsinge in Sweden. These are a simplified
version of the Short Twig runes but look very
different as some of the lines (staves) have been
removed. They would have involved much less
carving so inscriptions could be done much more
quickly, but they aren't so helpful to the rune
researcher – as you might imagine, the lack of staves
makes them harder to translate.

THE ANGLO-SAXON FUTHORC

The runes used in Britain during the 5th to 11th centuries are clearly based on the Elder Futhark but differ slightly from the original. Changing pronunciations mean we call the system a futhorc rather than a futhark but otherwise the majority of the runes are the same.

This futhorc is also referred to as the Anglo-Frisian Futhorc as it was used by the people of Frisia, a land encompassing parts of modern-day Netherlands and Northern Germany. Competing hypotheses suggest that either the runes came to Britain via Frisia or they went to Frisia via Britain. There's currently no definitive evidence one way or the other so for clarity I'll stick with the term 'Anglo-Saxon'.

Rather than cut down the Elder Futhark, like the Scandinavian approach, the Anglo-Saxons took the opposite path and actually expanded their rune system. By some counts, there were up to 36 Anglo-Saxon runes but some of these only appear in one or two places, so scholars suggest that some of these are simply variations, rather than runes in their own right.

For example, the Anglo-Saxon rune poem – the oldest known rune poem (runic alphabet listed with a poetic explanation for each character) – includes 29 runes, but most scholars consider two of these runes to be variations on the same character. The broadest consensus is that we add four more characters to the 24 of the Elder Futhark, for a total of 28.

The 28 runes of the Anglo-Saxon Futhorc are:

ᚠ	ᚢ	ᚦ	ᚩ	ᚱ	ᚲ	ᚷ	ᚹ
f	u	þ/th	o	r	c	g	w
ᚻ	ᚾ	ᛁ	ᛡ/ᛄ	ᛑ	ᛈ	ᛇ	ᛋ
h	n	i	j	ï	p	x	s
ᛏ	ᛒ	ᛖ	ᛗ	ᛚ	ᛝ	ᛟ	ᛞ
t	b	e	m	i	ŋ	œ	d
ᚪ	ᚫ	ᛠ	ᚣ				
a	æ	ea	y				

LATER RUNE DEVELOPMENTS

Broadly speaking, use of the runes died out as European countries embraced Christianity. Slowly but surely, the Latin alphabet that we use today replaced the runes as the principle writing system. The exception to this was in Scandinavia, where the people converted to Christianity but didn't simply lose their old traditions, language and customs. Runes lived on in the Nordic countries and they developed in a number of ways.

Firstly, there was the development of a set of Medieval Runes. This was an expansion of the Younger Futhark back to a position where every sound, or phoneme, had a corresponding rune.

Generally speaking, at this time Latin was used as the language of the church, while runes were used for writing in the Norse language for secular matters. Even so, some prayers were written in runes, and there are examples of all manner of church artefacts that have been discovered with runic inscriptions, including bells and fonts.

Runestones, which were boulders inscribed with runes, usually to commemorate the feats of dead men, were a tradition that persisted into this period. One of the latest we know of was raised in honour of a Danish archbishop, Absolon, who died in 1201.

The Medieval Runes built on the Younger Futhark in a number of ways over a couple of hundred years. Initially, additions were made by using what are known as 'stung' runes. These are runes with dots added to mark a change in sound, usually from a voiceless to voiced sound. So, for example, the 'i' rune, 'ᛁ', becomes the 'e' rune, 'ᛂ', with the addition of a simple dot.

The Medieval rune set also mixed Long Branch and Short Twig runes from the two main variations of the Younger Futhark but for different sounds. So,

the Long Branch 'a' rune was used for 'æ' with the
Short Twig version remaining as 'a'.

The final set of runes, which brings us almost to
the present day, is the Dalecarlian runes or dalrunes.
These were used in the historical province of
Dalarna, an area of modern Sweden where the people
are known to be independent. They continued to use
runes from the 16th into the 20th century, mostly

to write their native language, Elfdalian, which is a language developed from Old Norse and still spoken by around 3,000 people.

These runes were developed from the Medieval Runes that went before them, but took on many of the Latin letters that would have been impossible to avoid. The earliest inscription of these runes we have dates to 1596 and, rather handily, states 'Anders has made bowl 1596'.

FUTHARK

Elder

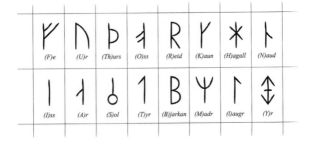

(F)ehu	(U)ruz	(T)hurs	(A)nsuz	(R)aido	(K)enaz	(G)ebo	(W)unjo
(H)agalaz	(N)auþiz	(I)saz	(J)era	(Ei)hwaz	(P)erþro	(A)lgiz	(S)owilo
(T)eiwaz	(B)erkano	(E)hwaz	(M)annaz	(L)aguz	I(ng)uz	(O)þala	(D)agaz

Icelandic

(F)e	(U)r	(Th)urs	(O)ss	(R)eid	(K)aun	(H)agall	(N)aud
(I)ss	(A)r	(S)ol	(T)yr	(B)jarkan	(M)adr	(l)augr	(Y)r

Younger

Long branch

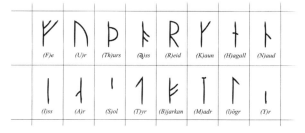

(F)e	(U)r	(Th)urs	(a)ss	(R)eid	(K)aun	(H)agall	(N)aud
(I)ss	(A)r	(S)ol	(T)yr	(B)jarkan	(M)adr	(l)ögr	(Y)r

Short branch

(F)e	(U)r	(Th)urs	(a)ss	(R)eid	(K)aun	(H)agall	(N)aud
(I)ss	(A)r	(S)ol	(T)yr	(B)jarkan	(M)adr	(l)ögr	(Y)r

Anglo-Saxon

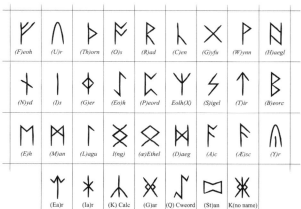

(F)eoh	(U)r	(Th)orn	(O)s	(R)ad	(C)en	(G)yfu	(W)ynn	(H)aegl
(N)yd	(I)s	(G)er	(Eo)h	(P)eord	Eolh(X)	(S)igel	(T)ir	(B)eorc
(E)h	(M)an	(L)agu	I(ng)	(œ)Ethel	(D)aeg	(A)c	(Æ)sc	(Y)r
(Ea)r	(Ia)r	(K) Calc	(G)ar	(Q) Cweord	(St)an	K(no name)		

DVÆRGERUNER
(Dwarf runes)

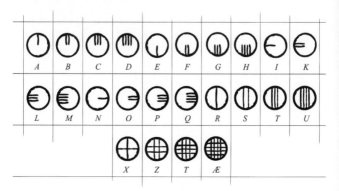

CHAPTER FOUR

WHERE DO WE FIND RUNES?

There are three considerations to the question, 'Where do we find runes?' Firstly, we must look at the kinds of objects and the kinds of situations in which we find runic inscriptions. Secondly, where in the world are they located? Finally, where in history were they inscribed – i.e. which Futhark are they inscribed in?

If you think about it, it's miraculous that we have any runes at all. Take a bracelet and bury it three feet down in a garden or a park. There's almost no chance that anyone will ever find that bracelet unless they saw you bury it, or you told them where to look. Thanks to the determined and systematic work of archeologists, archivists and runologists we have discovered around 6,400 items, of which at least 5,800 were found in Scandinavia.

Academic estimates of how many runic inscriptions were made in total can vary wildly. Without knowing how many people would have known the runes and were actively inscribing them, it's not easy to be more precise. There's a consensus that it's likely to be around 400,000, meaning we've uncovered around 0.1% of all possible runes.

We find runic inscriptions on many objects. Bracteates, fibulae, brooches, belt buckles and rings account for most of the jewellery and, of course, runes are found on coins. Weapons such as daggers, swords and spears have also been found with carvings.

There will always be gaps in our knowledge of runes because we can never find every rune ever written or inscribed. There may be hundreds, or even thousands, of objects perfectly preserved in the ground that will never be unearthed. More importantly, there are likely to be great numbers of objects that have been lost forever. Runes that were inscribed on wood or even bone will probably have decomposed by now.

This is, again, part of the reason why there is so much about the history of runes that we don't know. Every lost object – and every object buried in ground that has been built upon since – is a lesson we can no longer learn. If we had every rune ever written, we would know the answers to many of our questions.

Archaeologists work to unearth as much of the past as possible but it would be impossible to excavate the entire planet. Even narrowing it down to places where runes would have been used, that's still an immense area. But finds are made, through calculations, informed guesswork and a little bit of luck. Runologists study each item in very close detail, and each new item is a potential answer.

The Seax of Beagnoth is a large knife that's decorated with the only known complete inscription of the Anglo-Saxon Futhorc. Runes also appear on objects such as boxes and urns, often with imagery that combines to tell tales of legends such as Wayland the Smith.

Finally, there are runestones and, controversially, one inscription on a cave wall. The Kleines Schulerloch cave was discovered in Bavaria in 1937, but the runic inscription wasn't noticed until the 1950s. The inscription reads along the lines of 'Birg, beloved of Selbrad' and was thought by many to be faked. The discovery of a similar inscription in a grave in the early 21st century led many to reassess, but it's still considered suspect by most scholars.

THE ELDER FUTHARK

Inscriptions from the Elder Futhark have so far been found on around 350 items. The exact numbers are hard to assess because some inscriptions are alleged to be forgeries while some might simply be scratches that aren't deliberate. Of these items, more than 260 come from Scandinavia, and the remainder from further south, in Germany, Austria and Switzerland.

The location of artefacts can be useful in studying the spread of language but naturally there are problems with this. An object may be found buried in a place with a perfect inscription of who made it, when, where and why. But, even with that information, we still can't tell too much about how it came to be in the place where it was found.

The majority of the Scandinavian inscriptions of the Elder Futhark are found on bracteates, accounting for approximately half, with a further quarter on runestones. In the South only one bracteate has been found and no runestones; the majority are on fibulae. These were large, ornate brooches used to pin heavy cloaks together and were much more popular in Germany than in the Norse countries.

Two words appear quite frequently in the Elder Futhark inscriptions: 'alu' and 'erilaz'. The former word – which is written ᚨᛚᚢ and represented by the runes

'Ansuz', 'Laguz' and 'Uruz' – doesn't have a precise and agreed meaning, but most scholars believe it was important as a charm word in runic magic.

Originally thought to have meant amulet, the most common association is with the word ale: as today, a synonym for beer. It could have meant protection from the harms of alcohol, or it could simply have been people writing about beer. Some scholars have associated it with a similar word in the Etruscan language, where it means dedication.

'Erilaz', on the other hand, is usually interpreted as 'magician', to denote a person who knows how to use the runes for magical effects. It's a potential candidate for an early version of the English word Earl so it may also have been used as a military rank. The word has been found on amulets, weapons and stones, and appears often enough that it's clearly an important word and possibly part of rune-magic lore.

THE ANGLO-SAXON FUTHORC

The set of Anglo-Saxon inscriptions consists of only around 100 items, excluding coins. Most of these were discovered in the Eastern parts of the British Isles, with some also scattered around Europe, especially Frisia. They range from personal items, such as combs, through pendants and other jewellery to weapons.

One of the most famous objects is a whale-bone casket called the Franks Casket, which is owned by the British Museum. Dating from the 8th century, this item is intricately carved and tells tales from the legends of Northern Europe, along with both Christian imagery and Latin imagery.

THE YOUNGER FUTHARK

As the primary Scandinavian runeset, it's no surprise that the majority of existing Younger Futhark inscriptions come from Scandinavia. Of these, a huge majority exist in the form of runestones. These first appeared as grave markers in the 3rd and 4th centuries, but most date from a very prolific period in the late Viking age, from 950 to 1100 CE.

Only 10 percent of the runestones we know about are found in Denmark or Norway, while the rest are found in Sweden. No one really knows why this is but it's likely that it simply caught on as fashionable to raise runestones in one area and this spread to neighbouring areas.

This explosion in the popularity of runestones is probably due to two factors. Firstly, as time went on, more and more people would be familiar with the runes as they spread in the population, handed down through the generations. Secondly, this period overlaps with the Christianization of Scandinavia.

Runestones from this period almost always carry a combination of traditional Norse imagery and the new Christian imagery. Animals and human figures often took centre stage, with runes written in banners around the edge. Some inscriptions read right to left but most read left to right.

As we discovered earlier, the Norse people didn't simply abandon their old ways as soon as the Christian church reached them. Rather, they incorporated the aspects of the Church's teachings within their own traditions.

One thing that changed was the burial of the dead. In the past this would have been on the homestead, with a small marker of some kind. Christian burials tended to be in church graveyards.

So many runestones were raised on homesteads as a tribute to the dead, in lieu of an actual grave.

One final inspiration for the increase in popularity of runestones could be a certain King Harald Blåtann, whose story we're about to hear.

CHAPTER FIVE

RUNES IN THE MODERN WORLD

From literature to board games, from video games to politics, runes still frequently pop up in the modern world. J.R.R. Tolkien was a scholar of Germanic and Norse culture, mythology and language and there are several references to runes in his work. *The Hobbit* uses a version of Anglo-Saxon runes on its maps: some say Tolkein's attempt to render Modern English in runic form.

By the time he wrote *The Lord of The Rings*, Tolkein had developed Cirth script, a language that used many of the shapes of the existing runes but used them for different sounds. In the books, the Cirth eventually develops into the more sophisticated Tengwar script, an ornate writing that will be familiar to anyone who has seen the *Lord of the Rings* movies. Throughout Tolkien's books, Cirth is used variously by Elves, Dwarves and Men.

There are also many board games and video games, such as RuneScape, which incorporate runes into their gameplay. The runes are rarely used as a language and are simply there to lend an air of mysticism to the games. Some people consider this use of runes to be a form of 'Norsewashing', where elements of Norse culture and mythology are added for aesthetic reasons rather than any connection with Scandinavia and its history.

Vikings are popular in video games.

Of course, any modern use of runes that isn't a literal representation of the old Norse, Anglo-Saxon and Germanic languages can be argued to be wrong or fake. But runes hold special interest to a lot of people and many like to attempt to 'translate' English into runic scripts. It's worth bearing in mind that – while this is unorthodox linguistically speaking – it

can be a fun exercise and can help people become familiar with the runes.

On one level you can simply transliterate the Latin alphabet to its runic equivalent. For example, this might give my first name as ᚠᚾᛀᚱᛖᚹ. This wouldn't pronounce anything like Andrew, however, it would be more like Ahndr-eh-w.

Because the Old Norse language was limited in its phonemes, we don't always have a rune that will make the right noise. The short 'a' sound that starts words like Andrew was simply not part of their canon. We can, however, tidy up the end. If we replace the 'ew' with a 'u' rune instead, we get ᚠᚾᛀᚱᚢ and this might have been pronounced as something like 'Ahndroo', which is close enough.

Runes also appear in some of the Viking costume dramas that are popular today. One of my personal favourites is in the Netflix comedy *Norsemen*, described by one critic as 'Monty Python meets Game of Thrones'. Known as *Vikingane* in Norwegian, the show is unique as it's filmed in both Norwegian and English, each scene filmed twice, so there's no need to dub it into either language.

The runes in the series feature most prominently as a form of bathroom book. When the Vikings are shown attending to their natural business, they often grab a stick inscribed with runes and start reading, before laughing at whatever is written. This may not be an accurate depiction of the past, but it certainly helps show how the runes might not always have been used for sacred or magical purposes.

One use of runes that anyone will have seen if they've used any kind of technology in the past ten years or so is the Bluetooth logo. Bluetooth is a technology that allows computers or smartphones and peripheral devices such as printers and headphones to connect wirelessly over short distances.

Its distinctive logo is a combination, or bindrune, of the 'h' rune, ᚼ, and the 'b' rune, ᛒ. The runes were chosen to represent the Danish King Harald Blåtann, known in English as Harald Bluetooth. Harald was the king who united Scandinavia and the implication was that Bluetooth technology would unite all devices through a common wireless technology.

Harald Bluetooth is also the source of one of the world's most interesting runestones. Raised at Jelling in Denmark, the stone is special in a number of ways. Firstly, it sits next to a smaller stone raised by Harald's father, King Gorm the Old, in memory of his wife. Harald's stone is raised in memory of both his father and mother and celebrates his unification of Scandinavia (even though this only lasted a few brief years in the 970s).

The Jelling stones are important for several

reasons. For one, they could well have prompted
the enthusiasm for runestones in Scandinavia
that started around the same time. They are also
considered the birthstone of the nation of Denmark,
as they contain the first explicit references to
its name, as 'Tanmaurk' on the large stone and
'Tanmarkar' on the small stone. Finally, Harald's stone
attests to his Christianization of the Danish people.
Denmark was the first of the Scandinavian countries
to move away from their pagan origins and embrace

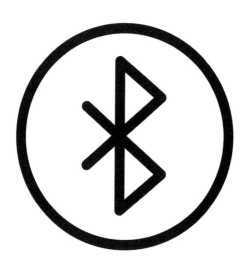

Christianity, thanks to Harald.

The inscription in full reads: 'King Haraldr ordered this monument made in memory of Gormr, his father, and in memory of Thyrvé, his mother; that Haraldr who won for himself all of Denmark and Norway and made the Danes Christian.'

Like many runestones, the Jelling stones would originally have been brightly coloured. While most of the pigment had worn away by the time they were discovered, enough evidence remained to recreate the colour scheme on plaster casts of the stone.

The stones were dedicated as a UNESCO World Heritage Site in 1994, and in 2008 they were covered by a glass case to prevent further deterioration. After so many centuries of Danish weather, they were finally showing signs of major degradation. Today, they remain in situ in Jelling, in their climate-controlled glass boxes. Coloured copies exist in Utrecht, Netherlands; London, England; and also in the Viking exhibition at the National Museum of Denmark.

Not all of our modern use of runes is as benign or worthy of celebration. In the early 20th century, the Austrian occultist Guido von List published a book entitled *The Secret of the Runes (Das Geheimnis*

Der Runen) in which he introduced a set of 18 runes, known as the Armanen Runes. These were based closely on the Younger Futhark, and List claims they were revealed to him during a spell of blindness following a cataract operation.

The Armanen were supposedly priest-kings of Aryan ideology. The runes became incorporated in the völkisch ideology, which had already taken the swastika as a symbol of German history. Völkisch ideology became intertwined with the National Socialism movement in Germany in the 1930s and so the runes were associated with German and Austrian nationalism.

Heinrich Himmler was one of the main members of the Nazi party who was interested in German mysticism and the occult. He adopted a number of the runes for use within the SS including the double-Sig rune that was its symbol.

Use of the runes died down after the end of World War II in 1945 but in recent times they have been co-opted once again by neo-Nazis and far-right nationalists. It's important when using runes to be mindful of the fact that, while they generally represent positive and powerful forces, some runes do also have this unpleasant connotation.

Of course, the most common modern-day usage

of runes is in the practice of magic and divination. Runes for many people provide an instant link to a powerful magical pool that allows them to experience the world on a level that differs from the regular day-to-day experience.

CHAPTER SIX

ODIN
AND
NORSE
MYTHOLOGY

Before we dive into the runes further, it's a sensible point to take a quick look at Norse mythology and particularly the role of Odin. Odin is one of the most important and revered gods in Norse mythology, especially in terms of the mythical history of the runes.

For much of the history of the Germanic and Scandinavian people, mythical tales were handed down orally through storytelling. Even the advent of writing systems didn't send people rushing to grab sheafs of paper to write down the stories. It was only eventually that writing became common enough that it was possible to do this.

A large part of what we call Norse mythology comes in the form of the two Eddas – the *Elder* or *Prose Edda* and the *Younger* or *Poetic Edda* – and various Icelandic sagas such as the *Saga of the Volsungs*. We owe a great debt to a learned Icelandic chieftain, Snorri Sturluson, who compiled the *Prose*

Edda, writing down the stories of how the world came to exist and the struggles of the gods in the Norse tradition.

The book we call the *Elder Edda* or *Poetic Edda* comprises the poems of the *Codex Regius*, a manuscript of unknown origin that was discovered in 1643 by an Icelandic bishop and sent to the King of Denmark as a gift. The Eddas have been translated into English several times throughout history and they're a must-read if you're interested in Norse mythology.

Even if you're not that into the subject, you've probably heard of Odin, Thor and Loki. We can thank the big superhero movies for their fame – and, surprisingly enough, a lot of what happens on the big screen is at least related to the original material. But, as with much of modern storytelling, the tales are much-simplified versions.

In Norse mythology, Odin is often called the
All-Father and depicted as King or Ruler of the gods,
although some liken him more to a messenger of
the gods, akin to Mercury or Hermes in Roman and
Greek mythology. Much of the confusion probably
comes from the inherent problems in mapping one
mythology onto another. While there are similarities
between characters and events in Norse myths and
those of the Romans and the Greeks, there are also
many differences.

Odin is associated with wisdom, and he is
said to have exchanged an eye for the chance
to gain knowledge, so he is always depicted as
having one eye. Depictions also usually include a
long, white beard and his famous spear, Gungnir.
Animal familiars, or companions, play a large part
in Odin's life, and he's often accompanied by his
two wolves, Geri and Freki. He also has two ravens,
Huginn (thought) and Muninn (will), who bring him
news from all over the world of men. Odin's final
main animal companion is his horse, Sleipnir, an
eight-legged steed that he rides across the sky and
between the realms of men and the gods.

Some key background to the runes is the mythical
explanation of how the Norse universe came to be.
In the beginning there was a chaotic nothingness
surrounded by ice and fire. As these two elements

met, the god-like giant Ymir was formed out of the chaos between them. He birthed many other giants and was nurtured by a cow, Audhumla, who emerged from the melting ice. By licking the ice, Audhumla slowly revealed the first of the gods, Buri.

Buri then had a son, Bor, who married a giant called Bestla and together they had Odin and his brothers Ve and Vili. These gods then killed Ymir and created the world from his body. His blood became the water flowing in rivers and seas, his flesh became the Earth, creating landscapes and mountains, and – in the centre of the cosmos – grew Yggdrasil.

Yggdrasil is the world tree, which contains the Nine Worlds of Norse Mythology. The important ones for us are Midgard, the home of men, and Asgard, the home of the Æsir.

The Æsir were one of two families of Norse gods, the other being the Vanir who lived in Vanaheim. When we talk of Odin as the leader of the gods, we actually mean that he's the leader or ruler of the Æsir. Odin went by many names, perhaps most notably Woden in Anglo-Saxon, from where we get the name Wednesday (Woden's Day).

The story of Odin and the runes is part of the poem Havamal, contained in the *Poetic Edda*. The tree of Yggdrasil grows out of the Well of Urd, whose unfathomable depths contain some of the most powerful creatures in the entire cosmos. Among these were the Norns, who together decided the fates of all who lived within the Nine Worlds.

The Norns would carve mystic symbols on Yggdrasil's trunk and, from there, the fates would be transmitted through the tree to wherever they needed to be carried out. Watching from on high, Odin came to desire knowledge of the runes and the power that it would bestow. He set about learning these powerful secrets.

Odin knew that the runes would only reveal themselves to those who proved worthy and so he decided on a sacrifice. Forbidding any of the other gods from coming to his aid, he hung himself from a branch of the giant tree and pierced his heart, so his blood flowed into the water below. For nine days and nine nights, Odin remained hanging, balanced on the brink of death, until finally, the runes accepted his sacrifice and revealed themselves to him.

Armed with the runes, Odin became one of the most powerful beings in the cosmos, able to thwart his enemies, heal his allies and banish the forces of darkness from the world. It is said that, once Odin had the runes, he could change the fates. This is probably where we get the idea that the Norse people don't believe that fate exists, or that everything is predetermined.

The runes passed from Odin to men through another tale. The god Heimdall is often known as the father of mankind. He is generally depicted as watching over Midgard, alert for the coming of Ragnarök, the Norse 'end of days'.

In the 'Rígsþula' poem, Heimdall sires three sons, Thrall, Churl and Jarl, with human women. Thrall is a serf or slave, Churl is a regular freeman, and Jarl is a nobleman. These men go on to become the ancestors of those three classes of people. The story tells that, once Jarl was old enough to demonstrate his noble blood, Heimdall taught him the runes. This chimes with what we know about runes, which were – at least initially – the preserve of the elite.

CHAPTER SEVEN

RUNES
AND
DIVINATION

Many people wrongly see divination as an attempt to predict the future or as a form of fortune telling. But practitioners of the various divination methods will tell you that divination is actually just a process of wayfinding through life; a way to seek guidance for unknown paths.

Divination will work with your subconscious to help you find the right way to proceed. Often the hardest part in divination is working out what questions to ask to get the results you're looking for.

The historical evidence for magical use of runes for divination comes in three parts. It's never entirely clear that the stories are attesting to runes in particular but they attest to symbols associated with magic and divination.

The first attestation is the Roman historian Tacitus. Considered by many to be the greatest Roman historian, Tacitus wrote a number of works on the history of the Roman Empire. He also wrote

three smaller works: *Agricola*, concerning his father; *Dialogus*, concerning the use of rhetoric; and *Germania*, concerning the Germanic tribes of Northern Europe.

In *Germania*, Tacitus tells of the taking of auspices and the drawing of lots. A branch from a nut-bearing tree was taken and cut into strips. On each strip they carved a sign or symbol. These strips were cast down on a white sheet and then whoever was doing the reading – either a priest in a public reading or the head of household in a private reading – would look to the heavens while saying a prayer and pick three strips at random and interpret them.

It's unclear if this tale was set in the time of runes or not, so it may have referred to runic symbols or perhaps some earlier Germanic symbols that are lost to history. Either way, it's obvious that the drawing of these lots and an attempt to make sense of the future was an important ritual of life for the Germanic people.

The second possible mention of runes was from the *Ynglinga Saga* when Granmar goes to Uppsala for a sacrifice known as the *blót*. It talks of how 'the chips fell in a way that he would not live long'. Again, it's not clear that this refers directly to runes, as there was a known practice of marking chips, or pieces of wood, with sacrificial blood before shaking them and throwing them down.

The final mention is by the Frankish Archbishop Rimbert in his *Vita Ansgarii* – a story of his predecessor, St Ansgar, who was a missionary in Scandinavia in the 9th century. Again, he tells of drawing lots, this time because a Swedish King, Anund Uppsale, wanted to raid Birka. The lots told them that attacking Birka would be a mistake and they should choose somewhere else.

Again, this has no proof of a connection to runes, but it shows the practice of casting to discover the fates. Many practitioners of runic magic and divination believe that these stories show that symbolism and casting were important to the Germanic people. Even without direct evidence, it's unlikely that the practice would have ended with runes, given the name rune and its association with secrets and magic and the legends of how they came to be known, first by Odin and then by man.

WHY AND WHEN TO USE RUNES

There are lots of different methods of using runes for divination. Most people who are looking for a method of divination will find that one of several methods will call out to them and seem to be the best fit for what they need.

Runes offer almost boundless opportunities for divination as the interpretations can vary widely. Even if you pull the same three runes in successive three-rune spreads, the way you're looking at the runes, the way your mind is working at the time and the situation you're pondering can give you very different results.

It can be beneficial to receive a rune reading from an experienced or professional practitioner to understand the mechanics before you dive in for yourself. As well as guiding you on areas to think about or work on, they will also be happy to help you understand any aspect you are struggling with, either relating to your reading or to the process of divination in general. Seeing the process can help you decide whether the runes are what you seek.

Always be honest and explain that you're thinking of diving in for yourself. Most will be overjoyed that their traditions are spreading to more people.

Some people find the runes to be a little too open to interpretation, so if you feel like you need more strict guidance, another system might be better for you. But if you're looking for a way to work with your subconscious to help solve your problems, work out exactly what your problems are, or simply assess where your life is and where it's going, the runes will likely work well for you. As always, an open mind and the willingness to work with the runes is key. You should get out of the runes what you put in, and much more.

Although runes can be helpful when you ask them direct questions, they work best when you're looking for help with issues. The more open your issue, the more likely the runes are to help you find answers. So, for example, rather than using the runes to ask

the very specific question, 'Should I look for a new job?', you might use the runes to work out where your job situation is right now, where it's going and whether that path looks good or bad.

There are also different methods of using the runes. Some look to the past, present and future of an issue, some look to the current situation, showing obstacles and ways to move past them. Others are simply a way of working out where you are. If something doesn't feel right, or you feel you need a change, you can cast several runes all at once and see which ones might guide you towards those situations that deserve or require your immediate focus.

It's worth mentioning that runes do not necessarily stand alone in the world. Though they can be used in isolated contexts with good results, many people will prefer to incorporate rune work within a broader context of ritual and tradition.

Those who work well with crystals, for example, can use those skills to imbue their runes with desirable energies. People who follow more of the modern paganism and heathenry traditions will also feel they get more out of runes when they form part of a broader magic or spiritual process.

GETTING YOUR OWN RUNES

Unlike Odin, you don't have to pierce your heart and hang from a tree for nine days to get your runes. You will have to make some choices though.

Firstly, whether you buy a set of ready-made runes or create your own set. In Norse traditions, it is considered usual to make your own set, but this may not be something you can do due to time, expense or ability. A set of runes can usually be purchased fairly cheaply and many people report achieving satisfactory results with pre-made runes.

For many, however, the thought of using runes they didn't make themselves is counter to the whole idea of runes, and they worry that pre-made runes will not get the results they require. If you want to follow in the runic tradition and treat the runes with respect, you will need to make your own set.

Once you have decided to make your own runes,

the next choice you have to make is what material
to use. Runes can be made from rock or stone, glass,
clay, bone, wood, bark and many other materials.

Rune casters often find that a particular material
calls to them based on their interests in other areas
of mysticism. For example, those who feel strongly
connected to the earth might choose to make
runes from clay pottery or stone, while those with
a connection to water might choose pebbles from a
river or beach.

You may also need to decide how much of a purist you want to be. Strict adherents to Norse rune casting will tell you that runes must be made either of wood from a nut-bearing tree, as attested by the Tactitus in the 1st century CE, or from bone or antler.

One problem I have with this, as mentioned before, is that firstly we have no direct proof that Tacitus was talking about runes when he related the tale of the symbols and the nut-bearing tree. Some suggest that Tacitus encountered the Norse people before the Futharks existed, so his story must have been related to some other divination tool.

Another problem is that rune casting isn't fully described in any of the sources in the way we do it today. It is based on a lot of guesswork and assumption so I'd be wary of anyone telling you that: 'It strictly must be this', because that's almost certainly just a rule they've decided to hold dear to themselves.

People will also tell you that any kind of man-made material is automatically wrong. On the other hand, some will suggest that because the runes are sacred, they will instantly sanctify anything they touch.

Most plastics and paper will feel too lightweight and insubstantial, so they're probably best avoided on practical grounds. Some materials will require painting and varnishing to get the runes to stick on the surface. While some natural paints and varnishes are available, the easiest options for these will be man made too.

Once you've chosen your material, you need to gather or obtain enough to make 24 or 25 pieces of similar shape and size. They need to be large enough that they can be easily read but small enough to hold several in the hand at the same time. If you're collecting from nature, you'll want to make sure to do it sympathetically and without causing any damage.

When you've gathered your materials together, you're ready to start inscribing your runes: a process sometimes known as 'risting'. How you go about this will depend very much on what material you've chosen.

With wood, it's common to either carve runes with a knife or burn them with a hot piece of metal such as a hot poker or soldering iron.

Rocks and stones may take the most effort as you'll need to find something harder than the rock to use for carving the runes into them. You can use small handheld tools such as chisels to engrave the symbols, but this will definitely take time.

Glass will likely require etching to make hard-wearing runes. The shapes of all the runes use straight lines, which makes them easier to carve than curves, but it's still quite a tough task. As mentioned above, the alternative for hard or fragile surfaces is to paint the runes on to the material. You can use an acrylic paint and cover it with a layer of varnish to keep the runes from rubbing off when used.

Natural clay is one of the easiest materials to work with – there are some clays that you can fire in a home oven, or even that can be left to dry in the air. Clay is very malleable so it's easy to create similar or identical shapes, and you can inscribe the runes on the surface easily. Once fired, they will be durable for as long as they are treated well.

A blank rune is commonly used during divination to give connotations of mystery, fate and hidden secrets. If you do this, be sure to treat the piece the same as the rest of the set, in terms of varnishing for example, to make sure it doesn't feel noticeably different from the others.

Now you have a finished set of runes to be proud of, you'll need something to put them in. A smallish bag will normally do the trick, ideally with a big enough opening to get your hand in and out easily. A drawstring purse is ideal for this, preferably made from a natural material such as cotton or silk. Some might opt for a cloth-lined box, which can be bought or made easily, as this gives room to work the runes and also offers protection when they're being transported.

Finally, most rune users have a casting cloth to provide a kind of arena for their rune casting. This can be any fabric but the traditional suggestion is white or untreated linen. Other people opt for a nice patterned piece of silk or chiffon.

You'll want a square piece, at least 12 inches or 30 centimetres on each side. This might fold up and fit inside your bag or box with your set of runes. You could be tempted to use the cloth as a makeshift bag to carry your runes, though the tying and untying of corners may cause it to become too creased to work with.

The final step is to become accustomed to the runes. This can be a long, drawn-out process or it can be quick, depending on how you go about it. One method is to choose one rune each day and keep it with you. Pick one at random or take them each in Furthark order. Let it sit next to you or keep it in a pocket and see if it makes you feel anything.

You could, if you prefer to speed things up, simply set aside a smaller amount of time for each rune and do the same. This might result in a weaker connection with the runes or it may be all that is needed.

CHAPTER EIGHT

HOW TO DRAW OR CAST RUNES

As I mentioned before, often the hardest part when casting runes is coming up with the question that will lead you to the answer, or process of answers, that you need for your situation. Over time, this can become an instinctive part of the process, and experience will help you narrow your focus, so you know the types of questions that yield the best results.

Firstly, you need to lay your casting cloth out flat on a table. Usually this will be in a diamond shape, with the corners pointing to the cardinal points of the compass. Try to find a space where you can sit facing North, if possible, with the South behind you.

While you're laying out your mat, think about what you are hoping to get out of the runes. For many people, this process of laying out the mat is a ritual of mindfulness that gets them ready. Once your table is prepared, you can turn your attention to the runes.

You can either empty them out onto the edge of the cloth or take them straight out of the bag, whichever you find works best. Mix them well, randomly or in a way that feels methodical to you. You might, for example, want to swirl around a certain number of times, swirl in different directions, or simply shake them up to be as random as possible.

Work out a method that will move as many runes around as possible so you have the best chance of divine intervention but without damaging them.

Try not to touch the faces of the runes too much with the sensitive tips of your fingers to avoid guessing what rune it is and so prejudicing your cast. This should also be done with your head raised.

Some people will say a prayer to the gods while mixing their runes to try to open up a divine connection and create order from the chaos. Others simply try to empty their minds of anything other than the question at hand. You'll soon come to understand what feels right to you.

Once you're happy with the mixing of your runes, it's time to start drawing or casting. Some people use the word draw to mean picking runes one by one and placing them down systematically; sometimes this is referred to as a spread. The word cast is often reserved to mean picking a number of runes and throwing them down at random.

Of course, you can consider all these methods as 'casts', as there's no reason why the method of distributing the runes should change the results. Both techniques lend themselves to different circumstances and questions so the distinction may or may not feel important.

As with making runes, casting the runes can be as easy or as complicated as you'd like to make it. There are several different methods to cast runes and there's no one 'true' method when it comes to the runes. I shall cover some of the most common methods of casting or laying our runes and show which positions relate to what aspect of your query.

With practice and experience you may find that some methods yield better results, or that it depends on the question. You may also find that you get better results with certain layouts, or certain numbers, other than those used most commonly.

Finally, it's entirely up to you how you develop your rune work. If you have a favoured shape that's not typically associated with the runes, it might be worth trying it to see if that shape opens up different pathways and interpretations for you.

SINGLE RUNE SPREAD

This is the simplest of all spreads and offers the broadest possible answers. You can either cast your runes and pick one without looking, or simply reach into your mixed bag and pull one out.

You might use this for broad themes like setting yourself up for the day: the rune you pick might reveal something of what your day has in store for you.

THREE-RUNE SPREAD

Sometimes known as the 'Norns' Spread', due to its association with the three fates and past, present and future, this is one of the most common spreads that people consult when they're starting out or when they're seeking a simple snapshot of life.

From your mixed runes, draw three and place them on the table in order. You can go left to right or right to left but remember the relative order of the three runes.

Rune 1 is a 'past' position and relates to things that have brought you where you are today or things that have ended.

Rune 2 is the 'present' position and shows you aspects of your current situation and the place you find yourself.

Rune 3 is the 'future' position and this will show you where you're currently headed. Don't forget it's in your power to change this.

ALTERNATIVE THREE-RUNE SPREAD

If you feel like the Norns aren't affecting your life, and that fate might not be applicable, it's possible to interpret the three runes slightly differently.

Rune 1 is an 'overview' of the situation you find yourself in or it relates to the question you are asking for guidance on.

Rune 2 is an 'obstacle' position and relates to any challenges you will face in resolving your present situation.

Rune 3 is an 'action' position and can guide you to find the best course of action to come through the situation and improve your prospects.

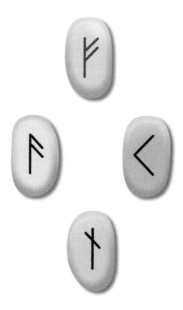

FOUR-RUNE COMPASS SPREAD

As the name suggests, for this cast you will draw and lay out four runes in the shape of a compass. Start with rune one in the North and proceed in a lightning shape so: North, West, East, South.

In a similar way to the Norns Spread, our first three runes tell tales or shed light on our past, present and future.

Rune four is an indicator of what will happen if

we continue on our current path. If the South rune is positive then things are going well with the matter at hand. A negative rune here is a sure sign to change course as soon as possible.

FIVE-RUNE SPREAD

Here we want to lay out a cross shape. Draw five runes. Rune one goes in the heart of the cross and the next four runes are placed West, North, South and East of the first in turn.

The runes at West, Centre and East across the middle represent the traditional past, present and future spread.

Rune three, opposite you, will tell you about obstacles to avoid, manage or, in some cases, simply accept.

Rune four, closest to you, usually gives you information about the resources that are there for you. A family-related rune in this position, for example, might let you know that it's time to reach out and lean on relatives for help with your situation.

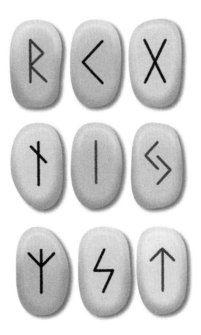

NINE-RUNE CAST

The final one we'll look at is our only pure cast. As the name suggests, we need to draw nine runes and cast them onto our cloth. Many attribute this method to the process Tacitus describes and so this may be the oldest form of rune divination known. It's not an easy cast to perform and it may take some time to get to a position where you can gain value from it.

Obviously, the runes don't fall into set positions and neat patterns when you cast them. It's how and where they fall that is the most important aspect. Runes that fall face-up and upright are the most important. The closer they are to the centre of the cloth, the more important they will be. Analyse from the centre of the cloth outwards. Start with the face-up and upright runes and try to decipher what the meaning could be.

Once you have dealt with those, turn your attention to those that are either face down or lying in an odd alignment ('merkstave'), either off-centre or sideways. Face-down runes might indicate that these aspects are not currently important to you, or it may be that they're hidden for important reasons. Merkstave runes often have very negative consequences and these will be dealt with in the next chapter.

Some runes are symmetrical, so they look the same either way up and have no merkstave. Others are simply so positive or represent concepts where a reversal or opposite doesn't make sense in divination.

The runes all have a meaning that was given through poetry but these are not the only meanings to the runes. Once we take the runes and apply them to the situation at hand, we may need to interpret them in some interesting ways.

For example, the literal meaning of 'Eihwaz' is horse. If you're pondering what to do about your horse, then this could be the right rune for you. It's likely, however, that if you draw the Eihwaz rune then it relates to something else – maybe a vehicle or transport; maybe a pet or other animal; or perhaps one of the characteristics of a horse such as strength, speed or trust.

You must always try to think laterally when you're interpreting runes. Sometimes you may be convinced that a seemingly unrelated rune means something that's not instantly obvious. If you have such a strong feeling, then that could well be your instinct kicking in, as it should. Try to look for a way to fit the rune to what you think it means, in the context of your situation.

Most people use the Elder Futhark for divination but with a couple of modifications borrowed from the Anglo-Saxon Futhorc. Firstly, the ŋ rune is of a more ornate form so it's easier to read. Secondly, there's a preference for the Anglo-Saxon definition of the c/k rune meaning torch, rather than the earlier definition of ulcer.

In the next chapter I'll take each rune in turn and try to give as much information as I can to help you with your interpretations.

CHAPTER NINE

RUNE NAMES AND MEANINGS

As well as being used to represent sounds in the early Germanic, Norse and English languages, many scholars assign names and meanings to the runes as well. How do they do this?

The Anglo-Saxon Futhorc runes and the Younger Futhark runes have poems that give a name to each rune in turn. As the two are roughly in agreement about the meanings of the words common to the two systems, it's assumed by some that those in the Elder Futhark are likely to have had the same meaning as those in the Anglo-Saxon Futhorc.

It's impossible to know whether this is a safe assumption. It's also impossible to know whether it was an earnest attempt to catalogue the names of the runes or simply an exercise, like writing 'A is for Apple', although there's a consensus that the meanings were genuine.

The table opposite gives a quick and easy guide to the simple meanings of the runes for you to refer to in a hurry.

Rune	Proto-Germanic Name	Meaning
ᚠ	Fehu	Cattle or Wealth
ᚢ	Uruz	Aurochs
ᚦ	Thurisaz	Thurs or Thunraz
ᚫ	Ansuz	God (associated with Odin)
ᚱ	Raido	Ride or Journey
ᚲ	Kaunan (Kenaz)	Ulcer (or Torch)
ᚷ	Gebo	Gift
ᚹ	Wunjo	Joy
ᚺ	Hagalaz	Hail
ᚾ	Naudhiz	Need
ᛁ	Isaz	Ice
ᛃ	Jera	Year
ᛇ	Eihwaz	Yew Tree
ᛈ	Perthro	possibly Pear Tree
ᛉ	Algiz	Elk
ᛊ/ᛋ	Sowilo	Sun
ᛏ	Tiwaz	The God Tiwaz/Tyr
ᛒ	Berkanan	Birch
ᛖ	Ehwaz	Horse
ᛗ	Mannaz	Man
ᛚ	Laguz	Water or Lake
◊/ᛜ	Ingwaz	The god Ingwaz/Yngvi
ᛞ	Dagaz	Day
ᛟ	Othala	Heritage, Estate or Possession
	Wyrd	The Blank Rune

The three ættir of the Futhark are usually attributed to three of the gods from mythology: Freyr, Heimdall and Tyr. Each can be considered as a set that works together with the others in harmony. They can also be considered as eight sets of three, with the first in each ætt working together.

If we look at the runes overall, we see that there is some repetition. For example, wealth and prosperity come up frequently, as does light in the form of the torch, the sun and the day. Drawing runes with the same, or similar, meanings can reinforce concepts quite strongly or, depending on position, they can show that, say, prosperity is fleeting or that the positivity you're experiencing will soon come to an end without some kind of change in course.

I've tried to stress that runes' meanings can be very personal. It's impossible to give every possible connotation of every possible rune in every possible combination because there are simply too many. As you work with them, you may find some of them take on special meanings for you above and beyond what is outlined here. So don't view the table as the 'right' answers, simply as a guide to get you started.

There are no right or wrong answers in rune divination because the runes are working for you, you are not working for the runes. It's up to you to find their meanings and apply them to yourself.

PART ONE
Freyr's ætt

The god Freyr is one of the most important and celebrated gods in all of Norse mythology, associated with peace, prosperity, good health, virility and good harvests. He's often depicted astride his boar, Gullinborsti, and with a large, erect member.

Freyr was a member of the Vanir gods but, after being a hostage of the war between the two sets of rival gods, he's also considered an honorary member of the Æsir.

The Germanic people would make wild-boar sacrifices to Freyr at weddings and other celebrations when the best chance for future success was sought.

He is especially associated with Sweden where, under the name Yngvi, he gave rise to the Yngling dynasty. Freyr is said to have inherited the rule of

the Swedes from his father, Njord, who inherited it from Odin.

After Freyr died, the Swedes pretended he was still alive, in an effort to keep his prosperity going. After three years of pouring his taxes into a hole in his burial mound, the Swedes accepted that so long as Freyr's body remained in Sweden the prosperity would continue. They decided not to burn his body and left him buried, instead offering blood sacrifices. Freyr was succeeded by his son Fjölnir and his descendants are detailed in the *Ynglingatal*.

The eight runes of Freyr's ætt – Fehu, Uruz, Thurisaz, Ansuz, Raido, Kenaz, Gebo and Wunjo – represent the important aspects of life on Earth and open up an initial connection between man and the divine.

One note on Freyr's ætt: some sources seem to attribute the ætt to his twin sister Freyja. The two are similar in character, both representing prosperity, fertility and fecundity. I can't find a definitive source to say whether it should be Freyr or Freyja but this makes sense to me in the context of the runes and their meanings.

NAME Fehu
OTHER NAMES Feoh, Fé
BASIC MEANING Cattle or Wealth
NAME PRONUNCIATION Fay-oo
TRANSLITERATION f
LETTER PRONUNCIATION /f/, like the f in Fur

Unless you're a farmer, it's unlikely that you'll want to take Fehu literally. But instead, start your thought process along the lines of wealth, success and abundance. This could indicate a project is about to come to fruition in a very profitable way. It could also mean that a change to your circumstances is on the cards.

In the olden times, cattle were a great symbol of wealth and prosperity. Those who could raise cattle had moved beyond simply providing for their family to being able to provide for animals too. This wasn't always easy in the harsh climate of Scandinavia and so Fehu is generally a symbol of success.

While it can relate to the tangible assets of money and riches, especially liquidity, it can also

relate to the consequences of that abundance. You could maybe expect to see enhanced social status, or improved health, come along with Fehu in your reading.

As the first rune in the set, Fehu is also associated with beginnings or new starts. Given that a new beginning could mark the completion of something else, it can serve as a reminder of the cyclical nature of life. Perhaps one underwhelming cycle is drawing to a close and you're about usher in a more prosperous one.

Besides prosperity or wealth, Fehu can in some circumstances relate to an abundance of positive feelings or experiences such as joy, passion or love. Relating back to Freyr, the god of fertility and fecundity, it could indicate positive news with regards to new arrivals in the family.

The position of Fehu can also affect its meaning. If Fehu lands in a 'past' position, it could signify a warning that prosperity is passing by and lean times lie ahead if you don't change your path.

Watch out for a reversal or merkstave Fehu in your reading. While it's not necessarily a bad thing overall, it could also indicate that a period of prosperity is coming to an end. Likewise, it could be an indicator that you're resting on your laurels and it's time to seek more challenging paths ahead.

Maybe it's time to cut your losses on something or tie up some loose ends that are holding you back. It could also mean, if you're in a period of prosperity, that it's time to share the wealth with others. The Anglo-Saxon rune poem specifically calls on men to share their wealth in the Fehu stanza.

While it's not necessarily always positive, Fehu is definitely an attractive rune to draw in most cases.

Fehu will bring riches to those who deserve them.

NAME Uruz
OTHER NAMES Ura, Ur, Yr
BASIC MEANING Wild Ox or Water
NAME PRONUNCIATION Ur-ooz
TRANSLITERATION u
LETTER PRONUNCIATION [u(:)], like the u in Bruce

The mighty wild ox, or auroch, of Northern Europe was a ferocious and fearsome beast. Possessing the same strengths of domesticated cattle, the wild ox adds an untameable quality to the themes of prosperity.

While Fehu points to wealth and prosperity, Uruz points to an untapped source of power that could just as well be equal to that wealth and prosperity. Some might consider Uruz to run in opposition to Fehu, and in some ways it can do that, but it can also be helpful to consider them as two sides of the same coin.

We need to consider the attributes of the wild ox: strength, stamina and determination. An Uruz in your reading could be a reminder that you have these qualities, and you need to keep going with

determination to reach your desired goal. It could also indicate that you've forgotten about the strength you have, and you need to work out how to get it back to make it through your current situation. This would especially be true if it was in a 'past' position on your cast or draw.

Perhaps it could be a reminder that you're not using your untapped potential and you need to make sure it doesn't go to waste. It's never a good idea to squander talent and resources if you want to achieve the best position possible.

Uruz might well be guiding you to ensure you're using your strengths, endurance and hard work in productive ways and not towards bad ends. That would especially make sense if you drew Uruz in an 'obstacles' position in one of the larger casts.

Beyond its meaning of strength, Uruz can also indicate health. Its determination aspect relates to mental health and the strength aspect relates to physical health.

Reversed, or merkstave, Uruz is almost always a warning. You may need to get your health checked out to be sure you're not in decline. Perhaps you're finding yourself struggling to cope with a workload and you need to summon the strength of Uruz to turn things around.

A reversed Uruz could be telling you simply that there are opportunities out there that you're missing, and you need to change your path to find them. It's certainly not ideal to have the strength of the Wild Ox working against you.

Uruz, the auroch, will help you reach the full potential of your power.

NAME Thurisaz
OTHER NAMES Thorn, Thurs
BASIC MEANING Giant or Thorn
NAME PRONUNCIATION Thor-ee-saz
TRANSLITERATION þ (th)
LETTER PRONUNCIATION IPA: [θ], like the th in Thor or sometimes IPA: [ð], like the th in Then

The famed god of thunder, Thor, wields his mighty hammer, Mjolnir. The hammer is so strong and powerful that Thor once had to dress as Freya and go through a marriage to a giant to get it back from where it was hidden.

Some say that the Thurisaz rune symbolizes the shape of the hammer. Others maintain it's a thorn on a branch. Either and both may be correct. What's surely true is that both the mighty Thor and the tiny thorn are strongly associated with Thurisaz.

Thor was well known for his frequent battles with the giants. As such Thurisaz is a rune of conflict. It's not always clear what form the conflict takes but if you search deeply enough you will surely find it.

Perhaps you're caught between opposing forces beyond your control, and you need to work out how to neutralize or placate both sides. Maybe you feel you're not in control and Thurisaz in your readings is calling you to stand up for yourself. There could be a clash that you're caught in the middle of, or a situation where others are controlling your life and you need to break free.

Perhaps Thurisaz represents a clarion call to galvanize you into protective action against an oncoming storm. Or it could simply be that there's healthy competition heading your way.

The conflict of Thurisaz could also offer an opportunity for cleansing or catharsis. It can appear in times of trouble to advise you that it's time to take the tough decision and let go of situations that are no longer working for you.

The dichotomy of chaos is that you never can tell whether a venture will rise or fall. It can seem that success is assured, only for failure to rise at the last minute or for victory to be snatched from the jaws of defeat. Thurisaz can tell you whether you're on the right path or whether you need to consider a change of course.

The thorn is a tiny and insignificant thing. Yet if it's stuck in your skin, it causes a pain that can't be ignored and shouldn't be endured. Thurisaz can indicate that you are perhaps overlooking some small problem that's approaching or minimizing something that will turn out to be a big deal. You could think you have everything in place but Thurisaz reminds you that you need to check the tiniest details to make sure no unexpected problems crop up.

Reversed or merkstave, Thurisaz lets you know how your feelings are affecting your position. It could indicate a helplessness or a sense of isolation as things play out around you.

There could also be some vulnerability that's holding you back from stepping into the fray and maximizing your opportunities. Or perhaps it's pointing out that you are fearing conflict and holding yourself back in a situation where you'd do better to take a more offensive position.

One thing's for sure, whether it's a thorn, or Thor, you're better off with Thurisaz on your side.

NAME Ansuz
OTHER NAMES Os, Oss, Aesc
BASIC MEANING God (associated with Odin), Message
NAME PRONUNCIATION An-sooz
TRANSLITERATION a
LETTER PRONUNCIATION IPA: [a(ː)] like the a in Far

We saw earlier how Odin, the all-father of Norse and Germanic mythology, is often equated with Mercury and Hermes as the messenger of the gods. While Ansuz is often translated simply as 'god', its association with Odin is undeniable.

Odin was both a relentless seeker of knowledge and also a tireless communicator. In this vein, Ansuz is primarily a rune of communication. If you find this powerful rune cropping up, upright and proud, in your reading then you're doing something right.

Communication comes in many forms and Ansuz relates to them all. Quite often its presence is referring to personal communication: how you think about and process ideas. Through intuition, reason and comprehension, you can see Ansuz as a rune of wisdom.

Be assured that Ansuz is on your side. It's reminding you that clear communication is the best way forward. Perhaps you are dealing with a situation and people are failing to come along with you because you haven't quite communicated things to them in the right way. This is simple to correct and will surely pay dividends.

In the 'past' position, it could be reminding you of previous times when you were able to use your wisdom to communicate in a positive way. Or it may be that the situation you are in relates to how you communicated in the past, for good or ill.

Ansuz is also good at reminding you to keep your communication lines uncluttered. Ensure you're not forgetting anyone in your correspondence or your thinking. You may simply need to focus on other people to resolve the meaning of Ansuz within your spread.

A reversal or merkstave of Ansuz is rarely a treat. There's something hinting at communication breakdown. Perhaps you're having difficulty making yourself heard in a work or home situation. Perhaps a friendship is toxic and you need to clear the air, or sort out another personal issue that's suffering from bad communication.

It's also common that Ansuz reversed is warning you to change your way of thinking and communicating to avoid risking offence or sending a relationship or a situation to a bad place.

Loki can often be found lurking around a reversed Ansuz too, so be sure you're on the lookout for tricks that may be heading your way.

Ansuz can help you unlock the power of intuition and communication, so be sure to heed it when it comes to your table.

NAME Raido
OTHER NAMES Rad, Reith
BASIC MEANING Ride or Journey
NAME PRONUNCIATION Ry-tho
TRANSLITERATION r
LETTER PRONUNCIATION IPA: [r] like the r in Ride

In modern times, many of us think almost nothing of travelling long distances. A couple of hundred miles in the car; a couple of hours in a plane: travel has become so quick and simple that the journey barely draws much thought at all.

Raido is here to change that. The wheel rune, Raido is concerned with all aspects of travel and journeys, whether they be physical or mental.

If you encounter the wheel in your reading, you should start to see that the journey is important. You'd be well advised to pay attention not just to the destination but how you get there.

It might refer to a real journey, if this is a source of trepidation, or perhaps a new route that is unfamiliar. Raido will prove to be a guiding hand

along the way to ensure that the journey will be, as far as possible, problem-free.

Raido will also help out on your spiritual journeys, ensuring that you feel confident that you have the mental tools you need, such as flexibility and an open mind, to help you reach your desired destination.

In a more abstract way, Raido could be an indicator or a warning that an upheaval is on the way. The journey could actually be one that arises through circumstance rather than one that's chosen.

If you are concerned with your career path, perhaps Raido is signalling that the direction you're moving is positive; you're gathering the necessary momentum, perhaps, to see a project over the final few hurdles.

Don't be too sure that the journey relates to you. In some positions, Raido could be advising you to look out for other people to help in their own journeys, either by something simple, such as offering a ride to a friend, or by more complex acts – like checking on your friends' mental health as they continue their journey through life.

The wheel itself is a powerful symbol of the constant cyclical nature of life. Raido can help you see that the best course of action is to simply ride the cycle, through its ups and downs, to find the smoothest journey overall.

A reverse or merkstave of Raido in a warning of impending danger. You might think twice if a real journey lies ahead of you.

In your spiritual journey, it could be that you're about to encounter some difficulty. Possibly there are some problems from the past that are about to rear up to throw your journey off course.

There's also a connotation with Raido in reverse of a stalled journey. Possibly you could be stuck in a rut in your working or personal life. Perhaps you need to take stock and evaluate what you can do to turn the rune round the right way and get your journey restarted.

Raido is a positive rune that will help you find the right path if you allow it.

NAME Kenaz
OTHER NAMES Kaunan (Ulcer)
BASIC MEANING Torch, Beacon
NAME PRONUNCIATION Kay-naz
TRANSLITERATION k
LETTER PRONUNCIATION IPA: [k], like the k in King

At many times in our human journey through history, the torchbearers have been among the most important people. They shed light on what is hidden, illuminate the path and help us avoid hidden dangers.

When Kenaz shows up in your reading it's a sure sign that brightness is around or will follow. Perhaps it represents some clarity on matters that have been hard to uncover or decipher. Kenaz can act as a guiding light through troubled times.

We can also see Kenaz in the context of bright ideas or inspiration. There may be some learning in our near future or a new understanding of the situation. Kenaz can represent the whole of the rune set, as the purpose of divination is to throw light on things that are hidden.

It can be congratulatory, showing you that you have succeeded in lightening the darkness, or finding hope or creative paths, and encouraging you to keep up the good work.

There's also a sense that Kenaz can be a moderating rune; have patience and all that is hidden will soon be revealed. If you're waiting for some important news, and Kenaz shows up in a 'future' position, it's a likely indicator that the news is coming soon and, often, that the news will be positive.

A torch can also represent a burning within. A passion for something that is driving you forwards. Be mindful of this and make sure you avoid extinguishing your inner flame and stifling your motivations.

Reversed or merkstave, Kenaz can be a harbinger of doom. Dark times may well be ahead and you should proceed with caution until you find a way to change the path you are on.

Reversed, it can also be a portent that things that you wish would be kept secret might be about to be revealed.

There's also a warning that there may be things that are deliberately being hidden from you. Perhaps a colleague or friend knows something that would be useful to you, and you should try to find out what that knowledge is, to get your torch burning brightly again.

Finally, perhaps a reversed Kenaz can be a sign that your inner flame – your passion, drive, motivation – is all in danger of being extinguished. This could be a very serious warning that, unless you correct your path, dark times are ahead.

Allow Kenaz to guide the way and you'll surely come to enlightenment.

NAME Gebo
OTHER NAMES Gyfu, Gar
BASIC MEANING Gift
NAME PRONUNCIATION Gey-bo
TRANSLITERATION g
LETTER PRONUNCIATION IPA: [ɣ] like the g in Guild

As well as being a part of our modern world, gifting has always been an important aspect of human existence. It's inextricably linked with festivals, celebrations and holidays, many of which have been around since the days when the runes were in use throughout the Northern lands.

Gebo's arrival in your reading is pretty much always a positive thing, as gifts are almost always a source of good – unless you lived in Ancient Troy!

Think of Gebo as a signal that things are about to improve. You may soon receive a gift as a tangible reward for working hard or for going the extra mile to help someone in need.

Romantically, of course, a gift could be involved in many ways. Perhaps Gebo is telling you that it's time to turn a relationship into a more permanent

union or perhaps it's time to expand a union with the gift of children.

Gebo can also be a reminder of the gifts that you possess internally. The unique set of skills that make you as a person should never be overlooked. If you're having a hard time with something, Gebo might suggest you already have what you need to turn the situation around.

Gebo could relate to gifts in broader terms. Perhaps a friend is in a position to offer you a work opportunity. You might also be able to give your time and skills to a collaboration or venture with others.

Gifting is an act of sharing so Gebo can point towards opportunities to share life with others.

There's no merkstave or reversal meaning for Gebo as the symbol appears the same in all directions. If it lands at a decidedly odd angle, it could be a suggestion that you need to focus on gifts. While it's not a negative, there could be something you're missing.

Perhaps you're not showing gratitude for help or assistance from others and need to start paying back. Or perhaps it relates to your innate gifts or talents that you have and how you could make better use of them in your current situation.

With Gebo in your spread, gifts abound for you and those near and dear to you.

NAME Wunjo
OTHER NAMES Wynn
BASIC MEANING Joy, Delight
NAME PRONUNCIATION Wun-yo
TRANSLITERATION w
LETTER PRONUNCIATION IPA: [w], like the w in Wonder

Joy in a hugely important part of our lives. From simple pleasures like starting a new book that we've been anticipating to huge joyful celebrations such as weddings or major birthdays, it's incredibly important to seek and maximize joy.

Wunjo, the rune of joy, can help us a lot in this regard. Probably the most positive of all the runes in Freyr's ætt (and possibly the whole rune set), Wunjo is a sure sign that, if joy is not currently in our lives, it will soon be arriving.

The symbol is often likened to a flag, perhaps as the symbol of a tribe or clan. This leads to obvious connotations of victory and the joy that vanquishing an enemy can bring. Enemies come in many forms, of course, so it could be a celebration

of the joy from, say, finishing a tricky project at work or successfully navigating a thorny issue in a personal capacity.

Along with this triumph often comes a sense of security as, once the problem is solved or the enemy trounced, we can relax. Wunjo in a reading can suggest it's time to relax and share in the joy of life with others.

Broader themes of success are incorporated within a Wunjo reading too. It could be a sign that work, or home life, is about to experience some joy. Maybe a promotion at work is on the cards, or a new baby may come along to bring joy to the family.

Along with joy, it's important to find a sense of balance. Wunjo can be a reminder to those with a chaotic life that seeking joy is now important. If you feel as if you're at the bottom of a serious problem and there's precious little joy to be had, Wunjo can guide you to find contentment with what you already possess rather than chasing joy in forms that might be elusive.

From an upright position as a powerful positive rune, the reversed or merkstave Wunjo is also a powerful portent, but this time it's predicting problems.

You could be about to experience a period of loss or despair. Sadly the reversed Wunjo is often hinting at the death of a loved one. It could also be less serious than this, but may still involve a massive upheaval such as a relationship ending or a surprise redundancy.

More simply, Wunjo could hint at obstacles looming on the horizon that need to be dealt with lest they cause stress, despair and a loss of joy.

It's not all bad news though. If you find Wunjo reversed in a 'past' position, this could be a sign that some major stressor or trauma is close to the end.

Heed the Wunjo rune wherever it appears, and joy will surely follow.

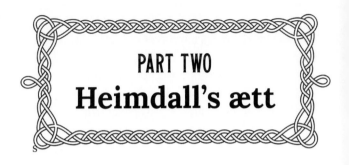

PART TWO
Heimdall's ætt

Sometimes called Hagal's ætt after its first rune – Hagalaz – the middle ætt is most commonly associated with the god Heimdall, who was the son of Odin and the Nine Mothers. He watches over mankind from his home in Himingbjörg, located where the rainbow bridge, Bifröst, meets Asgard, the home of the Æsir gods.

He also watches out for the coming of Ragnarök – the reckoning in Norse mythology featuring a mighty battle among the gods – that is foretold to end the current world and renew it afresh. His keen senses make him ideal for this task.

Heimdall is the sworn enemy of Loki, the trickster god. In his position as watchman, he often served as the foil to Loki's trickery. It's said that in Ragnarök they are destined to kill each other. He owns the mighty horn Gjallarhorn, which sounds throughout the realms, warning man and the gods of impending danger.

As the father of Thrall, Churl and Jarl (serf, freeman and nobleman), he is the originator of social class and is uniquely positioned to understand and protect the affairs of man.

The eight runes of Heimdall's ætt – Hagalaz, Naudhiz, Isaz, Jera, Eihwaz, Pertho, Algiz and Sowilo – attest to the strong relationship between man and the divine. It is the ætt that deals most closely with problems, challenges and the difficult aspects of life.

NAME Hagalaz
OTHER NAMES Haglaz, Hægl, Hagall
BASIC MEANING Hail
NAME PRONUNCIATION Ha-gu-lahz
TRANSLITERATION h
LETTER PRONUNCIATION IPA: [h] like the h in Hearty

No matter how much planning we put into things, and no matter how much we try to mitigate problems, there are always some things that can come along and leave us powerless.

Hail was very much like this for the Norsemen. Unlike nourishing water or gentle snow, hail at the wrong time can pelt crops with relentless punishment, leaving a clan or tribe unable to feed themselves or their animals.

Hagalaz in a reading must never be ignored. It's usually a sign to strap in and prepare for a bumpy ride because some major upheaval is about to unfold. Like hail, the Hagalaz rune is both unpredictable and uncontrollable. Even if you can shelter yourself, you may not be able to shelter everything that is dear to you.

The chaos predicted by Hagalaz in a rune reading can take many forms. You may be about to receive, for example, a painful and unwanted diagnosis in health matters. Romantically a seemingly fulfilling relationship might be about to hit the rocks.

It may not be entirely bad. Hagalaz may simply be alerting you to a situation where you will need to weather the storm, knowing full well that you are capable of it. Your inner strengths will carry you through. If you can see that something

is on the horizon, you'll be ready for whatever transpires.

The position of Hagalaz can be important too. If it's in a 'past' position, then that's a bonus as it means that whatever has recently been altering your life could be about to take a turn for the better. If it's in an 'obstacle' position, however, then you're definitely going to need to summon as much inner grace as you can.

In a cast, if you throw the runes down and Hagalaz is near a positive rune, such as Wunjo, then it could indicate just a mild blip. If Hagalaz teams up with other negative runes, then you'd do well to prepare for the worst.

There's no reversal or merkstave reading for Hagalaz as it's already a negative rune. It is, however, possible to reverse the meaning of Hagalaz in some circumstances. If, for example, you use Hagalaz as a talisman, you can use it as a shield against the unexpected rather than as a spreader of ill.

With Hagalaz on your horizon, you'd best be prepared, as what's coming your way could change your life.

NAME Naudiz
OTHER NAMES Nauthiz, Nauthr, Nyd
BASIC MEANING Need, Hardship
NAME PRONUNCIATION North-iz
TRANSLITERATION n
LETTER PRONUNCIATION IPA: [n], like the n in North

Our needs play an important role in our lives. What we need provides the motivation for what we do and dictates how much energy and time we have left over once our needs are met.

Naudiz primarily reminds us of the importance of focusing on our needs and not letting them fall by the wayside. I like to think of Naudiz as a rune of reflection. If the rune crops up in your reading, you probably want to pause and start thinking hard about your needs. An imbalance between what you have and what you need is being flagged up to you.

Needs have several layers. What do you need to live a healthy and fulfilling life? And in turn, what do you need to get those resources? By peeling back the layers, you can find the answers inside yourself as to what needs are perhaps not being met.

The basic needs – food, shelter and clothing – are usually fairly easy to meet, but on top of these we have other needs that maybe aren't being met. The need for connection with other people, for personal passions, or for time to spend on things other than subsistence living.

The appearance of Naudiz could be about employment, for example. You may be working, and that work may be fulfilling the needs for, say, food and shelter. But is it the best work you can be doing? Is it providing you with more than just your basic needs? It could be time to look at making a change.

As well as needs, there could be a connotation with boundaries. Perhaps some boundaries you have set have become distorted and you've allowed people or situations to encroach on your needs. It's important to remember that you should give freely of yourself but not more than you can spare. The needs of others are important but never more important than your own.

The rune of needs can also be a simple wake-up call. If you're struggling with a situation that perhaps you shouldn't be, Naudiz can remind you that you actually have everything you need but you may need to look deep inside to find it.

Opinion is divided as to whether there's a reversal or merkstave position for Naudiz. It's clearly an asymmetric rune so there should be, but many think that its slightly negative meaning prevents this.

My own opinion is that, when Naudiz appears merkstave, it's signalling something that's not exactly opposite but simply different from its normal meaning. Look towards other people and find out whether there are some who are preventing you from meeting your needs. Perhaps some are making it seem that they're helping but they are in fact hindering.

It can also be a warning not to confuse wants with needs. You need food and shelter but you don't need a 60-inch television. Don't allow greed to cloud your thinking.

Naudiz will open your mind and help you reflect on how best to meet your needs.

NAME Isaz
OTHER NAMES Is, Isa
BASIC MEANING Ice
NAME PRONUNCIATION Ee-seh
TRANSLITERATION i
LETTER PRONUNCIATION IPA: [i(:)], like the i in Ice cream

In the winter, nothing useful grows. In the modern day, we have in many ways cheated winter and can enjoy the freshest summer fruits and spring greens all year round. It's a time when we can still celebrate, gather together and enjoy feasting and warmth from the fire.

In days gone by, the winter was much more negative. The ice would arrive, and nothing could be done. If the harvest had been bad, it was a very precarious time until the ground thawed and the Earth returned to productivity.

If you find Isaz in your reading, the meanings are generally on the negative side. Start thinking along the lines of frustration and not being able to get

things done. Perhaps you've done everything you can towards a goal and are at the mercy of others before you can carry on.

If your Isaz arises with more specific runes such as Raido or Fehu then maybe you need to be patient and wait for a journey or an opportunity to come your way.

Isaz in a 'past' position could be the bringer of Spring and fresh starts in life. If it is prominent in your 'future', then you should prepare for delays.

On a more personal level, Isaz could be calling you to look within and find out whether some inaction is causing the situation you're asking about. Maybe you've reached an impasse or maybe your own indecision is holding you back.

Still, there's beauty in the stillness of winter.

Isaz could simply be advising you that it's time to slow down and take a break. Perhaps you've been overstretching yourself and Isaz reminds you that a rest could be in order.

As another negative rune, there's no specific reversal for Isaz. In a merkstave position, perhaps rotated, the meanings will probably be strengthened. Watch out for serious delays in your home or work life and expect to feel major frustration coming your way.

The merkstave position may also indicate that the ice of winter is coming at you from forces outside your control and that other people are set to be responsible for your period of inaction.

The rune of Isaz signals times of restriction; this may help you prepare and navigate them well.

NAME Jera

OTHER NAMES Ger, Ior, Ar

BASIC MEANING Year, Harvest

NAME PRONUNCIATION Yair-ah

TRANSLITERATION j

LETTER PRONUNCIATION IPA: [j], like the Germanic soft j in names like Jan and Jarlsberg or y in English words such as Yogi

An abundant harvest can be the difference between life and death when you live in the cold lands of the North. Even though harvests affect us only a small amount today, themes of abundance are still important in our lives.

Jera is the most positive rune in Heimdall's ætt. It almost always signifies good things on the horizon. It also acts as a reminder of the natural cycles of life and how we interact with them.

Harvest time is when we get to reap whatever we have sown. It's a reminder that we must make sure we're harvesting at the right time. Have our plans really come to fruition? It can challenge us to think about the results of our work and how we can maybe do better in the next cycle.

When Jera appears in your reading, think of all the connotations regarding a harvest. Just as the harvest is the natural conclusion of the growing cycle before plants die off for the winter, so Jera signifies the end of a cycle. This could be something obvious like a project drawing to a close and ready to provide the payoff you've been working towards. Perhaps there's a promotion on the way as a just reward for a consistent performance in your employment.

If you're a little earlier on your journey, the Jera rune arising could signify a successful graduation and transfer to a new school or out into the working world.

Closure is also an important theme of Jera. The end of a cycle can bring an end not only to successful journeys but also to painful experiences. If you have suffered a trauma, Jera could signal that you will soon be rewarded for the hard work you have put in to get over it with some personal release.

Finally, it's important to remember that death is the ultimate end to all cycles. While Jera will rarely have this connotation, it could be that someone who has lived a long and fulfilling life will soon be released from this world. This can be especially comforting if your query involves those who are suffering in the pain of old age.

As a positive rune, Jera truly has no reversal or merkstave readings.

With Jera on your journey, you know that there are good times ahead if you stay the course and complete your harvest at the right time.

NAME Eihwaz
OTHER NAMES Eiwaz, Eihaz, Eoh
BASIC MEANING Yew tree
NAME PRONUNCIATION Ee-was
TRANSLITERATION ï
LETTER PRONUNCIATION IPA: [i:], like the i in Police or the ee sound in words like Keep

The mighty yew tree Yggdrasil sits at the very centre of the ancient Norse and Germanic myths. Through its branches, it connects the nine realms – of gods, elves, man, the afterlife etc. – into one cosmology. The importance of the Yew cannot be overstated in the legends surrounding the runes.

As the thirteenth rune, Eihwaz sits in the theoretical centre of the rune set, just as Yggdrasil sits at the centre of mythology. It's one of the characters that is used less commonly in written rune inscriptions and is said by many scholars to take on a more magical quality.

The rune, like the yew tree, has many mystical connotations. Firstly, there's the idea of natural

strength and permanence. Yew trees can live for centuries, taking part in the cycles of life, taking rain from the ground and returning it to the air to fall once again, nourishing crops.

The yew can also spawn daughter trees from its branches so, in a sense, its life cycle is endless. An evergreen tree with an endless life, it stands for the more solid and reliable aspects of life.

Eihwaz may also involve the idea of studying to gain knowledge that is hard won. If this rune arrives in your spreads, you might expect to have to knuckle down and work hard to resolve an issue, or to gain the insight and knowledge you need, rather like Odin hanging from Yggdrasil for nine days and nights.

Eihwaz has connotations of poison too. The yew tree is especially poisonous and has been used for purposes both good and ill. Some of the compounds have been used for centuries to poison enemies or to commit suicide. Other compounds have been used to develop drugs that fight cancer. Eihwaz is a double-edged sword in this way.

Its association with death is more akin to the idea of regeneration. Much as the tree can regenerate after death, to live on through the next generation, so it might be hinting that it's time for you to let go of the past and allow a new beginning to take hold.

The strength of Eihwaz can also hint at encouragement. If you are currently questioning whether your current path will pay off the way you want it to, Eihwaz can confirm that your hard work will, eventually, lead to fruition.

It's not possible for Eihwaz to be reversed but it can lie merkstave, crossways, and perhaps indicate that the forces of chaos are coming to shake things up for you and that things you thought were permanent may be coming to an end.

Rely on the strength and power of Eihwaz to guide you in your journey.

NAME Perthro

OTHER NAMES Peorth, Pertho

BASIC MEANING Unclear; possibly pear tree, pear wood or an instrument

NAME PRONUNCIATION Pear-throw

TRANSLITERATION p

LETTER PRONUNCIATION IPA: [p], like the p in Potato

Of all the runes in the set, Perthro is the most mysterious. No one can truly attest to a meaning to the word. It doesn't seem to relate to any known words from Old English, Old Norse or any of their Germanic predecessors.

Some place the meaning as 'pear tree' or perhaps 'pear wood'. The symbol itself is reminiscent of a cup that has been turned on its side to spill its contents. Perhaps it's a cup used in casting runes themselves and Perthro is the holder of all of the secrets.

In divination, we think of Perthro as the interplay between concepts such as luck, chance, destiny and fate.

One lesson we can take from Perthro is about harnessing the powers that we have. Combine the

qualities we have gained through years of effort, trial and work with the natural qualities we were born with. Perthro invites you to accept what you can't change and save your energy for those things that you can.

As a keeper of secrets, Perthro may be letting you know that it's time to be more open with other people. Perhaps now you can tell someone a secret that you have been keeping.

On the other hand, the rune might be there to let

you know that there are mysteries you can't know yet but that will be revealed to you over time.

A reversed or merkstave Perthro may be something to fear. Your secrets may be in danger of being revealed by malign forces around you. It's possible also that you're not meeting your potential and are squandering the opportunities derived from your nature.

With Perthro the mysterious rune in play, life will certainly be interesting.

NAME Algiz
OTHER NAMES Eolhx, Yr, Elhaz
BASIC MEANING Elk/ Moose, Sedge
NAME PRONUNCIATION El-jeez
TRANSLITERATION z
LETTER PRONUNCIATION IPA: [z], like the z in
Zoology

The Elk is a familiar animal in Northern Europe and
across the world. Known as the moose in North
America, the Eurasian Elk is the largest member
of the deer family. It's known for its imposing
appearance, capped off with large antlers. The
sedge, meanwhile, is a popular grassy shrub with
broad, sharp leaves.

Algiz is commonly associated with both of these,
which have similar connotations. The antlers of the
Elk and the leaves of the Sedge are both important
symbols of protection.

Also associated with Algiz is a sense of power.
The Elk is a mighty and powerful animal, and it
can protect itself from most predators it's likely
to encounter. Likewise Algiz offers a powerful

protection, and some believe it signifies that the deities are on your side.

But although you should feel comfortable and safe with Algiz in your reading, don't be complacent and test that protection too much. Even if the gods are keeping you safe, they aren't likely to put up with you being reckless.

There are aspects of awakening in a spiritual

sense that are also associated closely with Algiz, through the idea that, if you are safe and protected, you are free to look deep inside yourself without making yourself too vulnerable.

If you receive a good offer when Algiz is on your side, you should feel free to follow it as you're almost guaranteed a favourable outcome. A new job, or a chance to work closely with a friend or colleague should be something you relish.

Beware of a reversed or merkstave Algiz as you're probably heading towards some hidden danger that you're not ready for. It's not necessarily a sign you're likely to come to harm but a suggestion that you might pay closer attention to your surroundings until you're sure whatever was hidden has been revealed and dealt with.

It's also possible that, on a spiritual side, reversed Algiz is pointing towards a loss of faith in your own intuition. You may need to search inside yourself and learn how to listen to those gut instincts that can often guide you well. Perhaps your protection from harm is being damaged by a lack of self-confidence. You might be allowing fear to rule your life, leaving you vulnerable.

Algiz will protect you from harm, so long as you don't take it for granted.

NAME Sowilo
OTHER NAMES Sigel, Sol
BASIC MEANING Sun, Radiance
NAME PRONUNCIATION So-willow
TRANSLITERATION s
LETTER PRONUNCIATION IPA: [s], like the s in Solitude

There are few more positive symbols in the world than
the sun, which brings light, warmth and joy, and banishes
darkness and cold. Sowilo, the sun rune, is similar. If you
have Sowilo at your table, you're in for a good time.

Your first thought on encountering Sowilo will
be vitality. The sun replenishes energy so you can be
sure that, if you have queries around health, there's
good news on the horizon. The sun is associated with
the life forces and will bring a boost to those who
encounter Sowilo.

In times of difficulty, such as work problems,
Sowilo suggests you will be able to resolve them ▢ to
find the light at the end quicker than it seems.

Sowilo is related to Kenaz, the torch, but
whereas the torch only illuminates a small area,

Sowilo brings light to all, even those that are in the shadow. With Sowilo around, it's difficult for things to remain hidden.

Sowilo can even work with your life forces to banish darkness from inside your soul. If you're having troubles that you can't get over, Sowilo may be the answer to letting the light free you from your troubles.

Sowilo in a 'past' position can show that you have been doing well in your life and, without any contradicting runes, that is likely to continue. It leaves you ideally placed to take advantage of your own skills so think along the lines of innovation and creativity and seize any chance to take a leap of faith into the unknown when you're travelling under the light of Sowilo.

There's no reversal or merkstave on Sowilo. It's universally positive, though in some cases it could offer a warning. You must guard against becoming complacent and ensure you are using your energies towards the best goals.

If your light is shining in the right place, then Sowilo will amplify it.

PART THREE
Tyr's ætt

The god Tyr is originally one of the most important in all of the Germanic traditions. Tyr is mentioned using the name Mars by Romans when referring to the Germanic gods, which is how we know he must have been of similar significance.

Believed by some to be another of Odin's sons, Tyr's parentage is not entirely clear as some also say that his father is the giant Hymir. Tyr is a god of war but also a god of balance and righteousness. He sees that war is fair and that justice is served. Tyr is often said to be the one who chooses the winner in battles.

Tyr is usually depicted as having one hand, thanks to the mighty wolf Fenrir. When Fenrir was born, the gods were amazed at how quickly he grew. Understanding that they couldn't let him roam the world freely, they tried twice to tether him and keep mankind safe, but he broke the bonds each time.

On the third attempt, the gods called the dwarves to forge the strongest chains ever. The dwarves created Gleipnir from magical ingredients including 'the sound of a cat walking' and 'the breath of a fish'. This created bonds that were stronger than iron but as thin as ribbon.

These chains made Fenrir suspicious, and he refused to be bound unless one of the gods put their hand in his mouth. Tyr was the only volunteer and, perhaps predictably, once Fenrir realized that he couldn't escape from his bonds, he bit Tyr's hand clean off.

The eight runes of Tyr's ætt – Tiwaz, Berkanan, Ehwaz, Mannaz, Laguz, Ingwaz, Othala and Dagaz – attest to the world of war and justice and of inter-relationships between humans. It is unique among the three ættir as it contains rune names for two gods – Tiwaz and Ingwaz. Both of these gods encourage humans to be the best they can in their affairs with each other.

NAME Tiwaz
OTHER NAMES Tewaz, Ti, Tir, Tyr
BASIC MEANING The god Tiwaz/Tyr
NAME PRONUNCIATION Tee-was
TRANSLITERATION t
LETTER PRONUNCIATION IPA: [t], like the t in Teepee

Every Tuesday, we unconsciously dedicate to the god Tyr as the 'Day of Tiwaz'. The romance languages celebrate Mars (in the form of Mardi or similar) and this connects Tyr and Mars as two gods of war who can guide us to victory

If Tiwaz appears in your reading, it will start your thinking along the lines of honour, valour and battles well fought. Perhaps you're coming to the end of a project or a natural cycle in life and Tiwaz is here to help you claim the win.

Tiwaz in some positions could simply be a guide that you're on the right path and that victory will come eventually, even if it could take a while.

If you are involved in leadership, either at work, within a family structure or even in a volunteer capacity, carrying Tiwaz with you ensures your thinking will be rational and logical and you will lead people to success.

The rune is often said to represent the more masculine side of things, in contrast to Berkanan's feminine energy, so if you're a female consulting the runes then Tiwaz could indicate that the matters are concerning the men in your life, be they family, colleagues or friends.

Tiwaz could even in some circumstances indicate that romance is on the cards or that a relationship is ready for moving onto a different level. Consulting the runes about affairs of the heart can be a challenge but if Tiwaz appears then it's definitely positive and passionate news.

Reversed or merkstave, Tiwaz is ready to make you examine yourself. Initially you might think that it means defeat is assured, and sometimes that will be the case. But it could simply be a nudge to examine your situation and try to find a way to get out of a rut or turn things around for a better outcome.

Tiwaz in reverse can also be a sign that your leadership is ineffective, or you are failing to convince people of your goals or the way you will achieve them. In family terms this could be a sign to open lines of communication and find ways to convince others that you are on the right path. It may also be necessary to re-evaluate your methods and find ways of achieving goals that others will buy into more readily.

Tiwaz can drive you to victory but only if you help yourself along the way.

NAME Berkanan
OTHER NAMES Bjarkan, Beorc
BASIC MEANING Birch
NAME PRONUNCIATION Bear-kah-nan
TRANSLITERATION b
LETTER PRONUNCIATION IPA: [β], like the b in Banana
but slightly softened towards a v sound

The birch tree reminds us that even the darkest
times must come to an end. As one of the first
trees to leaf in the spring, it's a symbol of renewal,
refreshment and the return of successful times after
a long, dark winter. The tree was sacred to the twin
gods Freyr and Freyja.

Berkanan will come into your reading at times
when you need a reminder of the positive aspects
of life. In fact, it stands as one of the most positive
runes available and gives us much help.

Associated with matters of womanhood and
femininity, it can often be seen as the counter, or
the flipside, of Tiwaz. As the mighty birch, Berkanan
signifies growth, especially after a long period in

the dark, so might symbolize that tough times are coming to an end.

As might follow from this, Berkanan also suggests fertility and for some relates to birth. But birth is not always literal. If you're trying to conceive and Berkanan appears, joy may soon follow, but it could also relate to more metaphysical matters such as the birth of a new idea or venture.

One more principal association with Berkanan is the idea of nurturing. There could be a confirmation that your efforts at nurturing are paying off. This could of course be friendships and relationships that you're nurturing, not simply young children.

In Berkanan, there is an inquisitive aspect to this though. You might want to take stock of how you are using and nurturing energies. Are you pointing them at the right target? Are you allowing time to nurture and nourish yourself? Are you open to receiving nurturing from others?

A reversed or merkstave Berkanan is not necessarily a harbinger of doom but it's likely that things aren't all as well as they might seem. You could be stagnating or failing to heed the signs that renewal is needed. Family matters could become tense if Berkanan is working against you.

Finally, in practical matters, if you are trying to conceive then a reversed Berkanan could be a hint that you're trying too hard, or it could, sadly, be a bearer of even worse news.

Berkanan will guide you or the women in your life to vitality.

NAME Ehwaz

OTHER NAMES Eoh

BASIC MEANING Horse, Steed

NAME PRONUNCIATION Ey-wahz

TRANSLITERATION e

LETTER PRONUNCIATION IPA: [e(:)], like the e in Emphasize

The horse has been one of humankind's most reliable and trusted companions through much of history. Horses are strong and stable when domesticated but show their wild side when left untamed. Many of our achievements owe much to the unique combination of human ingenuity and the strength of the horse.

Ehwaz, the last of the animal runes, represents all aspects of the relationship between humans and our equine partners. Horses allow us to make progress and Eihwaz represents a good place to start.

Unless you keep horses, the truly literal meaning is the rune will be of little use but the horse's connotations with journeys – and so progression

through life – can be represented when you find
Eihwaz in a spread.

If you're planning a journey, you can be sure
of a safe and pleasant one and of avoiding many
pitfalls along the way. Likewise, as you make your
way through life, Eihwaz can help confirm whether
you're travelling down the best path at
any moment.

Remember that horses can turn swiftly and so Ehwaz might be hinting that something is actually not right, and your course needs a swift correction.

One other aspect of horses that we can't overlook is that, while in the past they enabled much more rapid movement than we could manage alone, nowadays the horse has been superseded in most of our transport by faster options. For this reason, Ehwaz might show up if you're feeling frustrated with your progress.

Perhaps things are moving too slowly? This rune can be a reminder that if you're on the right path you simply need patience.

As with all runes involving travel and transport, Ehwaz reminds you not only to travel safely but to enjoy the journey. It's suggesting that you relax and don't worry too much about the pace. Like in the tale of the hare and the tortoise, slow and steady will win the race.

A reversed or merkstave Ehwaz is cause for some concern but it's not likely to be too destructive. Start thinking of ways in which conflict is delaying your path or you're maybe allowing others to let you down.

If you're asking about relationships, either in romantic or platonic terms, a reversal of Ehwaz could be a sign that someone in a relationship is not pulling their weight. You might need to re-evaluate and see how you can convert this drag on your journey into forward progress.

Ehwaz will help you on your journey but you must also be willing to pull your weight.

NAME Mannaz
OTHER NAMES Mann, Mathr
BASIC MEANING Man, Human, Person
NAME PRONUNCIATION Mahn-az
TRANSLITERATION m
LETTER PRONUNCIATION IPA: [m], like the m in Magistrate

'No man is an island, entire of itself,' said the poet and clergyman John Donne. A person doesn't exist without the efforts of mankind, both before their arrival on this earth and for the duration of their stay. Without the help of others, life would be almost impossible.

The Mannaz rune represents mankind in this way. It speaks to the interconnectedness of all humans, past and present. Thanks to the humans who lived before us, we no longer have to spend our days hunting our own food, and we no longer have to starve if the weather is unkind to our crops.

When Mannaz arises in your readings, you will instantly turn to thoughts of the other people in your life. You are the centre of a web that emanates from you, and Mannaz will remind you that, whether you connect to three people or 300, those connections are important.

Try not to see Mannaz as an indicator that there is something wrong with your connections. While this may be the case, it may be a reminder simply that humans do indeed need each other. Perhaps you have lost touch with old contacts and Mannaz is reminding you to reach out.

In personal relationships, Mannaz could well indicate that your bond is indeed strong with your partner, though be aware of the consequences if it has shifted to a 'past' position.

Everything human is up for grabs under a Mannaz rune. All that sets us apart from the animals – such as our conscious thought, our sense of fun and our creativity for its own sake – can be lines of enquiry, introspection and even celebration under Mannaz.

Mannaz can, however, also hint at some sort of friction arising between you and the world around you, especially if you're already feeling a disconnect forming between you and society. This would be a perfect time to see what might be causing that friction so you can reconnect.

A Mannaz reversal, or merkstave, is hinting at serious issues in your relationships with others. You

may be on a path that will lead to depression and isolation from others. Work on your relationships at all costs because they are so vital to your wellbeing.

It could also be a signal that the problem lies with others and it's time to take a break from a friendship or relationship that's not nourishing you as it should.

Let Mannaz connect you with others to make for a life that's more than the sum of its parts.

NAME Laguz
OTHER NAMES Lagu, Logr
BASIC MEANING Water, Lake
NAME PRONUNCIATION La-gooz
TRANSLITERATION l
LETTER PRONUNCIATION IPA: [l], like the l in Lamentable

Where water flows, life follows. In all of human history, water has been the underpinning of our development. From migration through valleys forged by rivers, to settlements by pools and lakes, water allowed us to do more with our efforts, to get more from the land.

Laguz stands for all of the things that water has to offer us. Not simply the flows of energy around and through us but also the wells deep within us. Expect to be dealing with your deepest subconscious if Laguz comes calling.

Our thoughts can begin with our emotions because these are the visible reminders of the depths below. If you encounter Laguz then you could be seeing great times within your emotional intelligence and maturity.

Laguz can also remind us to pay close attention to our instinct. Even the most rational and reasonable of logical thought can't solve all conundrums. If you find yourself on the horns of a dilemma and Laguz enters the fray, it's almost certainly a reminder that sometimes you have to follow your gut instinct and stop overthinking.

It can be too tempting to believe in one 'right' path – Laguz tells us to be mindful of the fact that even those we see as wrong for ourselves are still valid paths. All of our journeys lead to different places and we should choose paths that work for us but we should avoid judging those who are following paths that are different from our own.

One more relevant association is the relentlessness of water. This can manifest itself in a number of ways. In terms of perseverance, Laguz reminds us that a simple trickle of water can move mountains if it stays the course. It also reminds us that sometimes we need to allow ourselves to be swept along if the forces of Laguz are carrying us, as they will rarely lead us to ill ends.

Beware the reversal, however, as allowing yourself to be guided by a merkstave Laguz is certain to cause you problems. Water that ceases movement quickly stagnates, so you can think about ways in which your life might have come to a halt that you may not even have noticed. Perhaps you are stuck in a rut that is comfortable and you need to find new outlets for your imagination and creativity to enhance your prospects.

You might well be experiencing problems with your instinct and listening to what it is telling you, or you might be misinterpreting that instinct.

Allow Laguz to nourish your subconscious and be the invisible hand that guides your instincts.

NAME Ingwaz
OTHER NAMES Ing
BASIC MEANING Uncertain; usually taken to mean the god Ingwaz
NAME PRONUNCIATION Ing-wahz
TRANSLITERATION ŋ
LETTER PRONUNCIATION IPA: [ŋ], like the diphthong ng in words such as Spring

Fertility is important for the progress of mankind and also for everything to do with the affairs of men. It's not just vital for the creation of future generations, we need it for our crops so we can reap what we sow, both literally and figuratively.

The fertility associated with Ingwaz is of a more male nature, though that doesn't necessarily mean it can't apply to women. Rather, it's a symbol of the need for virility in matters of fecundity.

Ingwaz can relate literally to matters of pregnancy and childbirth (probably more so than the other runes) but that's just a small part of its potential.

Certainly, if you're seeking to conceive, you'll be delighted to see Ingwaz in your cast, but Ingwaz may also be pointing us towards the process of developing

the projects in our life, be they work- or home-
related. Ingwaz can tell you, for example, whether it's
the right time to start a new challenge or whether
you should wait for better times.

Also related to birth, we find a call for patience in
Ingwaz. Gestation takes its time as the baby develops
inside the parent, and so Ingwaz may beseech
us to have patience and allow whatever situation
or process that's vexing us to reach its natural
conclusion. Just like a premature birth, rushing
a project can yield results but they're often less
favourable than if we allow the time required.

Outside the auspices of pregnancy, Ingwaz
can let us know of a healthy personal union that's

about to happen, such as a new love relationship. If Ingwaz moves towards the past, however, then maybe a relationship has run its course and it's time to say goodbye.

Ingwaz, as related to the gods, is an overwhelmingly positive and auspicious rune and as such has no reversal of meaning.

When Ingwaz works with you, you possess the spirit of a god and the ability to give birth to great ideas.

NAME Dagaz
OTHER NAMES Daeg
BASIC MEANING Day, Dawn
NAME PRONUNCIATION Da-gaz
TRANSLITERATION d
LETTER PRONUNCIATION IPA: [ð], like the th in Their
or IPA: [d], like the d in Daphnia

As sure as day follows night, the light follows the darkness. This never-ending cycle shows us much about the world around us and how to interact with it. It also helps us manage our time and our dealings.

The night is crucial and is needed to provide rest and closure but the most important affairs of humanity are those of the day. Dawn brings a renewed hope. The darkness is lifted and what was hidden may now be revealed. Dagaz leads us into thoughts of hope, renewal, and positivity.

When you encounter Dagaz in your divination, you can instantly sense a lightness. Distinct from the torch of Kenaz, which illuminates what is directly around us, and the brightness of the Sowilo's sun, which reaches the darkest parts within us, the dawn

sheds a light that brings forth new chapters.

It could be that you're ready to make a move and Dagaz is here to nudge you in the right direction. Or perhaps you're feeling despair and not sure when bright times are coming. Allow the day to shed light and bring you forth from your troubles.

The cyclical nature of the day – of chapters ending and beginning – is also tied up in a sense of timeliness. While the day always comes again, at some times our nights are short and at other times it seems as if they will last forever.

In the cold lands of the North, the winter days never really get going while the summer days never truly end. Dagaz is here to remind you that no matter how short your day may be, it's important to make the most of it and not squander your time.

Dawn is also associated with the crepuscular nature of twilight. Some creatures are only active in the certain kind of light that we seek at dawn and dusk. The quality of the light takes on a nature that allows us to see things in a different way. Certain shades of colours are enhanced, and certain shades are subdued. So maybe our Dagaz is leading us to look at problems from a different perspective and try to tune out what might be overpowering our thoughts to see if some other aspects bring themselves to the fore.

There is no reversal to the day, in either a literal or a rune sense. Time marches only in one direction.

Allow Dagaz to bring forth light at the end of the long night.

NAME Othala
OTHER NAMES Odal, Othalan, Ethel
BASIC MEANING Heritage, Estate or Possession
NAME PRONUNCIATION oath-alah
TRANSLITERATION o
LETTER PRONUNCIATION IPA: [o(:)], like the aw in Yawn

What are we without those who went before us?
Our heritage is vitally important: as individuals, as a
society and as a global community. What gets passed
down has great power to enrich us but it can also be
a burden. Not everything we inherit is of use but it
deserves to be treated with respect.

Heritage is the central theme of Othala and
so it suggests a journey with our nearest and
dearest. Think about those things that are passed
to the successive generations. Obviously, there's
generational wealth and the inheritance of money,
assets and possessions – and Othala certainly speaks
to the desire in all of us to keep past things sacred
– but it's also about intangible inheritances such as
traditions, values and customs.

Through Othala you might see that it's time to
examine your traditions, either to make sure you're

following them as you should or perhaps to make sure you're not following them out of a sense of duty to the past when they're no longer required in the present.

At their heart is a set of core values that often run in families. This can influence how we go about living our lives and the customs we follow; Othala sets us thinking about this in detail. There are many ways we can approach matters with respect for the past and for our core values but in a way that reflects the current times more accurately.

Of course, Othala could be taken more literally. If you find yourself close to your parents, either physically or otherwise, then it could be time to lean into that generational knowledge and see whether their wisdom can bring anything to bear on a situation you're facing. Conversely, if you find that you are separated from your parents, perhaps it's time to bridge the gap and see whether there is scope to rebuild a relationship or simply bring yourself physically closer to them.

A reversal or merkstave Othala could spell trouble in your personal and family life, particularly with regard to the older or younger generations.

In very real terms, inheritance is often the source of great family drama as it is almost always associated with the death of a loved one, when people may not be thinking with a clear mind.

Be sure to work your magic on your relationships with siblings or extended family if you're finding this reversal in your reading. It could be a sign that not all is as well with family matters, or even that you are the one who is causing the problem.

Othala will grant you what you need to pass down to future generations if you see it as your guide.

NAME Wyrd
OTHER NAMES Odin's Rune, the Blank Rune
BASIC MEANING Confusion, Secrets
NAME PRONUNCIATION Weird
TRANSLITERATION n/a
LETTER PRONUNCIATION n/a

The mystery inherent in the runes is, for some, ably represented by Perthro. For others, there's a need for a blank rune to demonstrate a different kind of secret. Hence this dedicated 'rune of mystery'.

The name Wyrd refers to the mesh of fates woven by the three Norns, Urðr, Verðandi and Skuld, usually taken to represent the past, the present and the future. At all points in any reading, the Wyrd rune represents an impenetrable veil. Some say you should instantly stop the reading because no more can be revealed when Wyrd is in play. If it's the first rune you draw, that's probably true.

Often, however, Wyrd will only be obscuring one aspect of the draw. If it's in a 'past' position, it could be that something in your past is holding you back,

but the runes feel it's best not to make clear what.

In an 'obstacle' position, however, it is perhaps at its most powerful. There is something in your way, but nothing can or should be revealed about it at this time. This is a sure sign that it's time to do some involved thinking. Reach deep into your mind and examine everything that could be a factor.

Wyrd is not simply a block of knowledge. It could be a potent symbol that fate is making its presence known in your life. Rather than keeping you from understanding your situation, Wyrd can be a reminder that even though man is usually able to change his path and improve things, some aspects remain predetermined.

While Wyrd can be frustrating, it can also signal protection. Some secrets should remain that way and some things should be left to chance or fate. If Wyrd shows up, it could actually be a signal that you may be on the right lines but perhaps approaching a problem from the wrong angle, and it's time to regroup and rethink.

The association with Odin leads some to equate Wyrd with Odin's quest for knowledge. Odin would stop at nothing to discover new things as he attempted to become the most learned of all. So maybe, after all, Wyrd is simply an encouragement to not give up in your search for enlightenment. Only you can decide whether to treat Wyrd as a warning, a protection or an encouragement but it's likely you'll know which, when the time comes.

Wyrd will help you, but you may not understand how.

It's only as you take the time to work with the runes that you will come to understand their meanings and their powers as they apply to your life and your situations. As I mentioned at the start, there are too many combinations to detail them all. The same is true of people.

We use the word individual because each of us is the sum total of our experiences and those of our ancestors. You are the only one, the single individual, who has walked the exact path to get to where you are today, and you are the one who will continue the journey into the future.

Hopefully, with the help of the runes, you will find a way to make sense of all of the options available and chart a course that brings success, joy and prosperity and steers you clear of the major upheavals that can beset even the most positive of lives.

AFTERWORD

This is the point where we end our journey together. Hopefully you will choose to continue on your path with the runes.

If that's an academic path, and you're interested in learning more about these fascinating inscriptions, there are many other books and resources that will tell you in much more detail about the runes of the Norse, Anglo-Saxon and Germanic people. You can also play around with transliterating words, phrases and names into Old Norse via the runes, even though it doesn't have much meaning in the modern world.

If you are continuing down the divine path, then again there are many seasoned experts who have written books more extensive than this one, going into greater detail about different methods of casting and drawing runes. Beyond this, runes are used in various rituals, and you can dive into the world of making runic talismans, rune staves and other such symbols.

Finally, if you're fortunate enough to be able to travel, I recommend visiting some of the runic inscriptions that are on view to the public. The British Museum has a collection of runes on show, as do many museums in Scandinavia. The Jelling Stone in Denmark is definitely worth a visit, as are the coloured plaster casts of it in London and Utrecht as well as the National Museum of Denmark. For runestones in general, Sweden is the best place to visit, and there are many guides available to help you track them down.

I hope I've shown you that studying runes can be sacred or studious but it doesn't have to be dull. Either way, I'd recommend, for anyone who is interested in reading more generally about Norse and Germanic mythology, you pick up a translation of the *Poetic Edda* (aka *Elder Edda*) and Snorri Sturluson's *Prose Edda*. They contain some great stories and can stand to be read and reread many times. Like the runes themselves, each reading offers something new.

INDEX